# Devil's Ink

"True to their form, as of the Devil, these blogs have brilliant insights into the diabolical dangers of the media and other technologies. As these blogs disperse to us wise perceptions into the fiendish shrewdness of the evil powers, Pugh arouses us with such trenchant lines as, 'religion is a rank amateur in the death sweepstakes.' Readers will leave this book with much more comprehension into malignancy than they began!"

Marva J. Dawn
Author of *Powers, Weakness,
and the Tabernacling of God*

# Devil's Ink

## Blog from the Basement Office

Jeffrey C. Pugh

Fortress Press

Minneapolis

Cover design: Faceoutstudio, Jeff Miller
Book design: PerfecType, Nashville, TN

*Library of Congress Cataloging-in-Publication data*
Pugh, Jeffrey C., 1952–
  Devil's ink : blog from the basement office / Jeffrey C. Pugh.
    p. cm.
  ISBN 978-0-8006-9814-0 (alk. paper)
  1. Christian ethics. 2. Good and evil–Religious aspects–Christianity.
I. Title.
  BJ1251.P84 2011
  241—dc22
                                      2010044877

The paper used in this publication meets the minimum requirements for
American National Standard for Information Sciences—Permanence of
Paper for Printed Library Materials, ANSI Z329.48–1984.

Manufactured in the U.S.A.

14 13 12 11    2 3 4 5 6 7 8 9 10

*For my students and teachers*

# Contents

# Preface

What if Satan kept a blog? Blogging is a new form of communication, after all, and evil has always been keen on using new means of propaganda to accomplish its purposes.

Of course, evil is elusive—difficult to discern and more difficult to define. Still, since ancient writers first put the Satan figure into the story of Job, or the serpent into the story of creation, evil has been the subject of much of our greatest literature, from fiction to philosophy. This vast output is testimony to the fact that the mystery of evil perplexes and puzzles us, creates daily struggles for us, and continually scars our existence. If we can imagine intentionality behind all the evil in the world—not hard to do—then the image of Satan blogging to his minions about the contemporary ways and means of evil is not much of a stretch at all.

The man most known for giving devils a literary voice in recent times is, of course, C. S. Lewis, in *The Screwtape Letters*. How can anyone write a book titled *Devil's Ink* and *not* risk the charge of drawing from *The Screwtape Letters*? Indeed, C. S. Lewis did such an effective job for countless readers that in some ways I was inspired by that text to think through *another way of looking at evil*. In composing this work, I have been concerned to do something different than Lewis's accomplishment. For this generation, not only has the medium changed—from letters to a blog—but the whole character and locale of evil has changed: *Devil's Ink* explores how evil arises in stealthy ways in popular culture.

Writing in the voice of Satan is risky. Though the tradition is as old as Genesis or Job, the literary conceit is difficult to pull off. John

Milton, Johann Wolfgang von Goethe, Lewis, William Blake, Norman Mailer, and hundreds of others have assumed this voice in order to make observations about human beings and to provoke readers to reflect critically on the charges the devil makes.

While the point of view expressed by Satan brings its own challenges, I hope it proves an engrossing and entertaining way of saying things about us from an entirely different point of view. Oddly enough, this device helps to open the space to ask questions of ourselves that we usually don't think about. It allows us to wrestle with whether the author is bringing things to our attention that call for deeper reflection.

Questions abound: How do we account for the presence of evil? What does evil have to do with idolatry? How does evil mask itself so that we accept it as a matter of course? How would we ever gain the ability to discern evil in our social orders? How does evil colonize our attitudes, habits, and thoughts? How do people of faith relate to their cultural contexts when those contexts seem so indifferent, or even hostile, to faith? These are some of the struggles I try to represent in this small book.

In this text, I also try to indicate some of the ways in which the forces and ideas to which we give our lives have material effects in the world. These effects often end up bringing us much misery. This is not a book about our personal relationship with sin, which can be defined in so many ways, as much as it is an exploration of *the ways that evil embeds itself structurally in human life*. Until we think clearly about how the choices we make construct architectures of imprisonment for us, we repeat patterns that have wounded our souls.

Is this too vague? Then think about the ways we hurtle toward our own destruction as a nation or a planet. Our economic and political orders all too often lead us to unsustainable ways of life or even to environmental collapse. As I write these words, one of the worst ecological disasters in human history is still being dealt with in the Gulf of Mexico. It is uncertain at this point what the long-term effects of that oil spill will be.

What impels us to construct our common life in such a way that we destroy it? The decisions are ours alone, but look at the results and you find much that scars the rest of creation. Is not Satan depicted in our imagination as a force of malignancy, resisting the good creation of God? Where are our habits of thought leading us then? Sixty years ago, Dietrich Bonhoeffer wrote:

> The huge masquerade of evil has thrown all ethical concepts into confusion. That evil should appear in the form of light, good deeds, historical necessity, social justice is absolutely bewildering for one coming from the world of ethical concepts that we have received. For the Christian who lives by the Bible, it is the very confirmation of the abysmal wickedness of evil.

This observation, from his *Letters and Papers from Prison*, has always resonated with me, in no small part because of when it was written, in the darkest days of Nazi Germany. It is difficult sometimes to see evil when one lives in the midst of it; it is usually in retrospect that one sees how evil manifested itself. Yet it is my hope that framing our reflections on evil in this creative way provokes in readers some questions and reflections about the great "masquerade of evil" all around us.

My debts in this text are many, some of which have already been mentioned, but some of the authors I was reading as I was writing this book need special attention because either their ideas, or my response to their ideas, found their way into these pages. Sometimes I used a specific illustration I read from them, such as Slavoj Žižek's story of the peasant and the witch, to drive the point. At other times, I am wrestling with ideas from a host of thinkers I have read and worked with through the years. If readers pay attention to the tags at the end of each entry, they will find other places I drew from to make my points. In order to help facilitate quick access to the tags, I have included a partial glossary for the reader. You are encouraged to do more research into the terms used.

These are fragments, offered for your reflection, and, much like a blog, do not offer a distinct narrative path. This is a book that should be read a bit at a time. Too much evil in one setting can be harmful to your health. I thought it might be interesting to experiment and set up a site where the readers can argue about the claims being made in this text. I hope that a community of responders will continue the conversation started in this book by visiting devilsinkblog.com.

I wish to express my deep gratitude to Michael West, as well as Susan, Marissa, Joshua, Olga, Will, and Mark, and all the other wonderful people who work at Fortress Press for all their help and attention in bringing this project to fruition. I am also grateful to Elon University and the Department of Religious Studies, where I fulfill my vocation to teach. I am privileged to have wonderful colleagues who generously teach me everyday. I also want to thank my car pool, who, on some mornings, were a little too eager to contribute to things Satan might say. Finally, as always, I am graced by the presence of my wife, Jan Rivero, who never stops believing. I would have said she inspired this book, but that might be misunderstood.

# Pleased to Meet You, Hope You Guessed My Name

You may wonder why I am starting this blog. The fact is, my colleagues, we must be flexible and innovative or we risk losing influence, and if there is one thing that I fear, it is losing influence. So I am taking this opportunity as another way of "catapulting the propaganda" (memorable turn of phrase, that). In the coming entries, I will be talking about our hopes and wishes for the success of our work and laying out our long-range strategic planning for the coming cycle.

I know you are uneasy because we have most influence when, like some government agencies, no one suspects that we exist. True power is that which doesn't call attention to itself. We have our goals to achieve and still hope to embed ourselves more concretely in the lives of the human creatures. There are markets among them we are seeking to acquire, and so, colleagues, we must be diligent.

I debated whether to start a Facebook page, but there are so many who are doing the heavy lifting for us there it would be merely redundant. I am also thinking about a Twitter account, but am still trying to figure out what the point is. Their celebrities and politicians are increasingly making use of it, so anywhere politicians are found, I suspect we will find something useful to extending our domain as well. As far as the tweets go, the instant gratification part is something we certainly understand, and the constant self-absorption is, of course, our stock in trade, but how much use could Twitter possibly be?

I know, we had a huge success with PowerPoint, but you can't get lucky all the time. Perhaps Twitter will turn out to be another way they endlessly amuse themselves, right into our loving embrace. Of course, they don't see the true problems until it's too late. For example, they create technologies of social interaction, but they bleed away the empathy from actual relationships as a result. Just think about how the hive mind functions to change the meaning of the word *friend*.

I must confess, I see the benefit of technology in ways I could not see before. This is one reason why I love the humans so. They create things that end up creating them instead and then don't see problems down the road. They run ahead of their ability to reflect morally about where their creations take them and then seem shocked when things blow up in their faces. We have extended ourselves deeply into their world through the words, "Wouldn't it be cool if we could . . . ?" You can complete that sentence with almost anything. Wouldn't it be cool if we could split the atom? Wouldn't it be cool if we could download consciousness into a machine? You see where this leads? For my part, I just want it to lead to their eventual extinction.

This particular blog, however, is for you, colleagues, so that you may have some insight into our long-range planning and strategic positioning among them. I hope you will find things that will amuse and enlighten you. Though our methods are timeless, we also have learned through the ages to use those fleeting and transitory things that humans have created to help us reach our goals.

Total-quality management means being flexible and responding to the environment. One must change with the times or risk being irrelevant, and if there is one thing I am not prepared to be at this time it is ignored. For strictly pragmatic purposes, however, it is of the utmost necessity always to be implausible in the minds of those whom we are seeking to influence. Above all, we must make sure that this information doesn't get leaked because we can see what happens when the truth about secret things becomes public knowledge. None of us wants that, I assure you. So, none of you better go all Julian Assange on me or I will have you for lunch—literally.

In the coming entries, I hope to answer your questions and update you on what my latest thinking is. As I said earlier, we must be nimble and flexible enough to respond to the ever-increasing opportunities we see in front of us every day.

POSTED BY BLZBB AT 7:01 AM, 02/01
TAGS: ROLLING STONES, *SYMPATHY FOR THE DEVIL* | GEORGE W. BUSH | FACEBOOK | TWITTER | WIKILEAKS

## The Heart of Matter

We actually only want space—lots and lots of space. We want room in the world. To that end, our desire is no different than for many of them—space to breathe, to feel free, to not be bothered too much by the demands of another, a little place to call our own. What was the term Adolf used about living space for the Germans? *Lebensraum*? We do want psychic as well as physical space, though. That seems to be the rub for some people. Well, that and the fact that there will never be quite enough room for us. We'll always want more. We should ensure they will always be wanting more as well.

We want the space to define them; we want to move into every area of their lives and have them define themselves by our logic, our thinking. It is remarkably easy, actually, but we must be careful not to overplay our hand. Sometimes ideas take shape all by themselves. We only need to tweak things slightly to ensure that our needs are met.

Take matter, for instance. Our opponent likes matter. This is hard to understand. It's just so *messy*. We can't grasp why our enemy wants to be embodied in life. Our enemy even infuses matter with sustaining life. So we must make sure that we keep this fact from those miserable creatures. Matter must be seen as entirely different than what we know it really is. Matter must be seen as just dirt, gas, and chemicals, nothing more. We certainly don't want them to suspect that our enemy is creating all this.

We have worked at this for quite some time and have achieved truly great success in having them define matter as something so far removed from our enemy that they do not even see our opponent exists within all material life. I'll have much more to say about this later, but for now, just one glimpse at a part of our larger project.

If we keep this from them, then they will not see the possibilities present in the material world and they will continue to abuse it in ways much to our liking. This is how we do our work. Take all that is given to them as a gift and distort it. It's not hard, actually, because they are so good at not being attentive to what is in front of their eyes. Curious how they can be surrounded by so much glory and yet willfully tune it out somehow. I mean, they are being rained upon by beauty, and yet they are so preoccupied they don't even notice it most days.

POSTED BY BLZBB AT 1:20 AM, 03/01
TAGS: SCIENCE | PHYSICS | ECOLOGY | *LEBENSRAUM* | *MEIN KAMPF*

# Desire

I know it is hard to believe when I claim this, but, seriously, I am a big fan of desire; it is truly one of the best instruments in our toolbox. I especially enjoy the way with them that desire becomes an inclination and once it becomes an inclination it often becomes a habit, and habits are hard to break. Desire often colonizes their souls by becoming rooted in their identities, and at that point they are ours. They don't even give a second thought to the trajectories of their lives. Sometimes desire becomes inscribed on their bodies. Vanity, greed, lust, envy, sloth—all of these have—how shall I put it?—earthly effects. As I said before, we want to have material consequences in any way we can.

Humans are full of desire, and thus irrational at their heart. In and of itself this is not a bad thing because our opponent created this in them, but in our hands, colleagues, desire can be useful. For example, in most moments the desire of parental love is something we find repugnant, but how often have we seen this legitimate and positive desire get distorted to the point where the child becomes an empty vessel into which parents pour all their ambitions and dreams? The human landscape is littered with the wreckage that this one distortion creates. Point for us, I should think.

There are other desires we are able to twist. This is why envy and resentment are much to our liking, especially when a victory can only be savored when one's most hated and feared enemies lose. It is sort of like the relationship between the fans of the New York Yankees and the Boston Red Sox: it is not enough for one's own team to win; the other team must lose. And if they lose badly, well, that's just icing on the cake, isn't it? What happens is that the foe, the rival, the enemy, comes to define them through distorted desire.

You know that story where the witch tells the peasant that she will do to his neighbor twice what she does to him? The peasant doesn't even think twice about it, but slyly responds, "Take one of my eyes." It's kind of like that. I love that story. Who says a story has to be literal to be true? This twisting of desire helps us to win space, and that fulfills *our* desires.

POSTED BY BLZBB AT **3:00 AM, 08/01**
TAGS: **PARENTS** I **BASEBALL** I **YANKEES** I **RED SOX** I **FOLK TALES** I **SLAVOJ ŽIŽEK**

## Desire and Suffering

Just one more word for right now. What I am sharing with you is one reason why Gautama the Buddha was close to true reality. When he said that all life is suffering (we wish!) and suffering is caused by desire, he was really onto something. When he said that stopping desire would stop suffering, he grasped a significant truth. But, see, here is where things can go our way. In the attempt to stop desire some humans take it too far and seek the path of self-denial. They can become so self-righteous in their single-minded pursuit of a life of nonsuffering that they deny themselves any pleasure whatsoever.

This becomes a desire all of its own, doesn't it? The desire to flee suffering by shutting off all desire can become a path that leads to much despair. Gautama recognized this and cautioned them to take the middle path between grasping after things and totally letting them go. Holding life and its impermanence lightly was sound advice. Appreciating what is at hand in the moment is wise, but who has time to cultivate that kind of discipline? *Attachment, detachment, I can't worry about this, I've got mouths to feed*, they think and silently slip into forgetfulness.

POSTED BY BLZBB AT 6:00 AM, 08/01
TAGS: BUDDHISM | FOUR NOBLE TRUTHS

...........................................................................

## Desire, Revisited

Though this seems like small stuff to many of you, consider the pattern that we use. First, there is the desire for something. We don't care what it is; we can use the desire and distort it for our purposes. Often the desires become inscribed on their bodies, but as I mentioned previously, these are usually the small things— vanity, greed, lust, envy, and sloth. You can even see it sometimes in the landscape of their faces.

Remember how I mentioned that even Gautama warned them about the way that desire becomes a controlling force. He knew that desire causes suffering because desire, undisciplined, becomes inclination and colonizes the soul by finally becoming identity.

Parental love is not the only thing we can distort. Take the normal desire of wanting to contribute something to the world. In and of itself this is not a bad thing, but notice how that desire becomes distorted among them. Sometimes the single-minded pursuit of the good can become a thing that swallows up the rest of their lives. They neglect those who love them or they ignore their own bodies. How many times have we watched as altruism bleeds into ambition? Desire works to blind them to the ways in which they shape their lives. Some things just become habits to them, and habits are hard to break.

This is especially true in the habit of thinking. Once you think a thing is true, it is notoriously hard to change a habit of thought. I would think the best evidence of this would be racists. There can be nothing more reflective of *our* world than hatred without reason. In them we find a hatred born of something so monumentally stupid it defies all logic. Once they have drunk the poison of racism, nothing can change their minds about their hatred, which, as you can see, suits us fine.

They seldom take the time to ask why they are so uncomfortable, so unhappy, so unfulfilled. There is something hovering at the periphery of their lives that calls them out of their imagined comfort to a different kind of life, but they fear that call to new life as much as we do. As long as we can keep this presence a thing to be feared, we can keep them from entering the type of discipline that writes in their minds and hearts another way to live. What they don't quite grasp is that the thing that beckons them, that wants them to respond, is our worst nightmare. I want to ensure that it is theirs as well.

POSTED BY BLZBB AT 4:00PM, 08/01

TAGS: RACISM | KKK | DALITS | JEWS | PALESTINIANS | HUTUS | TUTSIS | *INCEPTION*

. . . . . . . . . . . . . . . . . . . . . . . . . . . . . . . . . . . . . . . . . . . . . . . . . . . . . . . . . . . . . . . . . . . . . . . . . . . . . . . . . . . . . . . . . .

## The Bigger They Are and All That . . .

Some of you have written lately to say how pleased you are with the latest political leaders and their sex scandals. You said it must please me to watch this particular desire bring them down, even more so when they are so publicly pious. Well, sure, but really, I do wish you all would get a bigger vision sometimes. Sometimes I really do wonder if you are as clueless as they seem to be.

Yes, we are always happy when the likes of political leaders are so ridiculously oblivious about their own lives that they let themselves be blindsided by the overwhelming need to feed their egos. This is, in fact, one way we are able to use desire to our ends, but it's low-hanging fruit, really. We can knock off dozens of these before morning coffee.

By the time they get to this point, they have made so many compromises they are hardly aware of what types of corruption have been planted in their lives. Even that twit Augustine recognized their enormous capacity for self-deception. He told his fellow creatures they possess such vast depth and complexity they can't even begin to understand their own motivations, much less the subtleties of good and evil. But no one really listens to him anymore. Anyway, the point is, they don't really take the time to learn how truly self-deceptive they can be.

If we can just hide this fact from them, if we can keep them involved in so many things that they have no time to attend to their souls, they will usually ensnare themselves in all types of mischief. The fun part comes when the traps they set for themselves snap shut and then we watch as they act like animals trying to gnaw their legs off to escape from their folly. Good times.

It is easy to win space among them, especially those who start their lives hoping to "help" others. This altruistic impulse is another desire that they muck up. The ones who invoke this mantra early on in their careers actually mean it, but are of little consequence to us. How much bang for the buck is it to corrupt a city-council member, anyway? Sure, we keep tabs on them as their careers progress, but the tracks are so common by now. They start out idealistic (which, let's be honest, starts for most of them in high school student government), find they can get ahead by some small betrayal of a colleague or constituent, and then the path is set, depending on the hunger of their ambition and the lack of self-awareness.

The ones who really annoy us are those who seem to grasp that there are aspects of their souls that, if fed, would lead them into our waiting grasp. They are so disappointing to us because they become self-aware. They seldom make those small and seeming insignificant choices that pick at their souls, tearing apart the fabric slowly but surely until the whole cloth comes unraveled. Fortunately for us, most of the creatures are so busy they don't have time to think that much about their souls.

By the time Senator X, President Y, or Premier Z (I would have said King A or Queen B, but seriously, with royalty, what else does one expect?) hits the headlines to satisfy the prurient interest of the rabble, who really cares? It doesn't serve our larger interest, though I must admit, it is good for a laugh or two. The funniest part, for me at least, is when they are finally exposed for the narcissistic cretins they are and they immediately start to blame others for their decisions, "It was the thong she wore to work," or "He seemed to listen so carefully to me when I felt bad, not like my spouse." Pure comedy gold. Makes me laugh every time. At the moment of truth, they cannot see what is so obvious to all those around them.

As I said before, though, there are those who do cause us some concern. When the true ramifications of their behavior are finally uncovered for what they are—self-deception on a level they had not even suspected—they actually, and I hate using this word, *repent*. I don't mean by this the usual public show of confessing to some great sin, claiming they will never do it again, and then disappearing for awhile, later surfacing to run for public office. This amuses us. They have learned nothing about themselves and will be useful to us later down the line. There are plenty of those types to go around.

The ones who really get under my skin are those who come to realize that self-deception is like the air that humans breathe. These few realize they must constantly be alert to the justifications they use to authorize their actions, especially when they want so badly to legitimate what they want.

Those who acquire some sense of spiritual discernment are the ones to truly keep an eye on. They see more clearly what is at stake. Being burned by their own folly, they grasp the connections between events, people, and places that constitute the way they order their lives. The whole comes into focus for them. We don't like it when they see the bigger picture. We want to keep them focused on the immediate thing in front of them.

POSTED BY BLZBB AT 12:57 AM, 11/01
TAGS: POLITICIANS | AUGUSTINE | CONCUPISCENCE | *ELECTION*

..................................................................................................

# Don't Just Use, Abuse

Some of you (and I have your IP addresses, you little weasels) took exception to my last entry. You said, and I quote one of you, "But, Boss, aren't you being too cavalier about things like adultery? I mean, they make such a big deal of it; why do you brush it off?" Did I? What gave you that impression?

This is one of my greatest strategies—make what is of little consequence in the larger scheme of things the largest thing possible. I care about sex, of course, but not in the same way they do. I thought I had explained this. When one of them commits adultery they have already crossed so many lines of self-deception that the physical part is just icing on the cake to me. This is so common it's not that big a deal.

Moreover, when they simply use one another to fulfill their desires, this is really unimportant to my ultimate goal. It is what is larger in this action that is at stake. The sexual act itself, because it has been given to them as a gift from our opponent (and this really is a mystery to us, because what did they ever do to deserve something like that?), is not insignificant to my purposes, but not really of great concern to me when it remains on a private level.

This is not to say I don't like the pain inflicted when the inevitable hurts and betrayals come from using this gift stupidly and selfishly. And, of course, minions, we have the satisfactions of seeing some of their more pious ones go off the deep end about sex, but this is not really the most important thing to us. Well, I take that back. If their repressed lives blindside them later on down the line, that brings me much happiness. How many times have one of them ended up in some sleazy hotel room with a hooker and some coke and wondered, *How did that happen? We* know how it happened; the hilarity is that *they* don't, even though the evidence was right in front of them all the time.

Like I said previously when talking about politicians, they will make their public displays of contrition, but the way they continue to pursue power makes clear they have learned nothing. They will only become more vulnerable to their own self-deceptions in the future. It is not the individual and their sexuality that most concern us. If they want to bring pain into their lives by the way they use one another, the more the merrier, I say.

But the fact that they are *using* one another is something we have been able to build on for quite some time. This is when desire turns in on itself, and we have always been able to use that level of selfishness to construct other works that are testament to our influence. We had a great advance in this a number of centuries ago in what they call Western civilization. (It makes me smile a bit, really, this whole "civilization" thing; at the drop of a hat they are only too ready to annihilate one another.) They barely perceived the shift, but I became very interested because a door was opened to more than I could ever have imagined.

I am not sure of the exact time, but at some point the creatures seemed to arrange the orders that control their lives in a different way. Previously, their lives had been oriented in some ways around thinking about how humans *should* treat one another. Thus, they made some attempts, however feeble, to treat one another as worthy of respect and not see one another solely as ends to accomplish what they wanted. Or, at the least, they paid lip service to the idea.

But then, and here I have some theories, they started to order their lives not on the basis of how human beings *should* treat one another, but on how they actually *do* treat one another and how this behavior might be more effectively *managed*. It's not that they stopped thinking about morality altogether; it's that the entire moral dimension shifted.

I saw an opportunity because once they did this they became something other than human beings to one another. They became objects, and so things were measured in ways not done before. They became commodities, bought and sold among one another. They have always done this in a way, I suppose, if you look at how long slavery has been a part of their world, but now it seemed as if new possibilities emerged.

Do you see the connection I am making now with sex? As long as they *use* one another it serves our hopes for them. This utilitarian approach, when connected with their economic lives, gives rise to big things, like child prostitution and sex slavery. Human trafficking is something that we can really sink our teeth into because of the countless ruined lives and innocent souls we can destroy. It is only when their sexuality and its desires move into larger structures that we find it worth our time. There is still the small joy one gets when we see individual lives ruined through betrayal or abuse, but given what humans are with all their appetites—well, as I said before, this is low-hanging fruit.

What is one more politician or other public figure who ends in disgrace to us? I do enjoy seeing those who put these people on a pedestal become disillusioned, but that is minor. No, we should always have the big picture in mind, not the small stuff. Those individual lives ruined are just minor benefits on the way to our major goals of winning space in the world.

It is when they can buy and sell the most innocent lives as if they were pieces of meat without a second thought of the harm done or the lives destroyed that tells me that for all their supposed progress they have come a short distance indeed from the days they were scouring the ground for food to eat. We take far more space in their sophisticated commerce than we do in some sleazy hotel room.

The best part of this is that they will relentlessly focus on the part we care the least about. The media will be full of someone's weaknesses and everyone will be consumed by the scandal. The real scandal, though, continues in the darkness where the light seldom shines. If they were to make as big a deal about human trafficking as they do about some peccadillo of their celebrities, we would become far more nervous. That might actually change the world, and I can't have that.

POSTED BY BLZBB AT 4:00 PM, 13/01

TAGS: UTILITARIANISM | SEX TRADE | THAILAND | TED HAGGARD | BILL CLINTON

## Obsession with Possession

Some of you in your responses to me about the last entry and the ideas I was trying to communicate have asked if I enjoy the use of freedom to enslave them in the erotic. Why in my name are you so obsessed with sex? It's like you were a member of the C Street Fellowship or something.

I want them to define freedom so that they construct the world in such a way that others become objects to them. You remember how this works, or at least you should. Once persons become objectified, they will do all manner of harm to one another. Objectify a person and it is not too long before you can put a price on them. Then they are moved around as part of capital, like cows. This is the way the world goes around, isn't it?

This is how pornography operates, actually. Some of you are happy that pornography is so dominant in their lives, but sometimes I think you don't really get the beauty of it. We are pleased when people live out of different desires than what our enemy wants for their lives. The freedom offered in pornography is the freedom to possess the object. The idea of possession is usually hidden from them (see self-deception), but it is an underlying aspect of their obsession with pornography.

It is imperative in the absolute and endless exposure of all sexual acts that we keep from them the aesthetic and authentic beauty of the erotic. If the pornographic is always that which must be possessed and exposed, then the truly erotic is something else entirely.

The best way to kill the positive and spiritual energy of sex is to make it so free it becomes the weapon of choice in their relationships. The passion can bleed pretty quickly out of them if their partner is withholding sex. There is, of course, the opposite strategy of having the puritanical killjoys who see all sexuality as pornographic define sexuality for society. If the neo-puritans can just convince the world that all sexuality is narcissistic self-absorption, then we win. If our company is truly fortunate, the creatures will never be able to see our opponent's hand in sexuality at all.

I want to keep from them the fact that spirit infuses matter with desire and that the whole of existence is in some sense the eros of our enemy. I want them to see matter as empty space that they fill with whatever content they desire. I don't want them to see matter as potentially sacramental. If they ever learn to see existence as the embodiment of our rival, our side loses.

It makes me miserable when they realize that matter itself can mediate the presence of our enemy. It drives me crazy when they grasp that authentic freedom can be found when one binds oneself to another. It is when they learn to live truly erotic lives that I want to puke. Who could stand to live in a world like that? Who would want to? What would you do with all the unused neon lights?

If they see too clearly the fact that love and sexuality are parables for a deeper love than we bring to them, then the other person is no longer their fantasy, their image or ideal, not even an instrument to be used. If they begin to see one another clearly, then other persons exist in all their complexity, inscrutability, mystery, and yes, even irritability. Because an authentic drawing near to another means that all the flaws, foibles, and really dark parts are there in the bed (or the field, forest, or sea) with them. How our enemy reveals hopes and desires for them through those types of exchanges makes us really suspicious and not a little anxious. We don't understand it. It's not the way *we* do things.

Oh, one final word today. As I pointed out earlier, the true joy of the pornographic is that it is built into their economic structures. Because they want to maximize profit at all costs to human welfare, the system creates the conditions for pornography to be a growth industry. How pervasive do you think it would be if they could not make money at it? The way our enemy set this up really means sex can be kind of boring. Who wants to bother with commitment?

We must work to prevent them from seeing that divine love can be revealed in that act in a way like no other.

POSTED BY BLZBB AT 7:09 PM, 14/01

TAGS: C STREET FELLOWSHIP | SOHO/LONDON | AMSTERDAM

........................................................................................................

## Snowflakes Stacked on One Another All Look the Same

I want to follow up on something I shared with you earlier. It is not that the individual is totally unimportant to us; she is just not that vital to our long-range strategic planning. I know those little twits make much of the individual and how important each and every person is, but in truth they don't really mean it. Otherwise, why would they so constantly be willing to sacrifice the individual on the altar of larger concerns when it is expedient?

The individual is important when it serves their purposes and not a moment longer. Look at the way their political orders are arranged. "We stand up for the little guy, the individual," they say, until the "little guy" has an idea of his own that conflicts with their plans, and then it's all "Shut up in order to allow the common good to prevail." But, look who is defining what the "common good" is—it's usually those who hold power.

We have seen this all through their time on the wretched planet. We have been able to use this misplaced concern to great effect. Think of the countless dead before their time because the "collective" became the absolute. Once you make the whole the absolute, you make the individual an abstraction whose only reason for existence is to serve the collective. Of course, they always argue their case for mass murder on the basis that they are helping the "common man."

One of our most successful strategies is using this in their public life. How many countless millions died in service to the "people"? We are especially happy when their political orders start to accuse the ones they oppose of not caring about the individual, when, in fact, none of them do. These types of deceptions become so simple, even brutal and effective, that they accomplish our ultimate goal of annihilating those little cockroaches. We can stand back and watch them kill countless millions in the name of the individual. Remarkable, really. And we haven't even gotten to the really good stuff yet.

POSTED BY BLZBB AT 2:05 PM, 15/01
TAGS: STALIN | MAO | CRYSTALLINE FORMATIONS

## Like Anyone Cares

Just another word for now about the individual. We are actually able to use this idea for our own purposes, especially in their religious life. If we can just make them focus on the individual, then *all* their concern becomes about them and their "relationship" with "god" (I realize this term "god" is just their feeble way of trying to express what we here in hell know all too well. I'll make sure to use scare quotes so the slower among you will understand not to take this too literally. Besides, I don't want to give our enemy too much respect.)

This overwhelming concern about their own lives plays directly into our hands because then we have them right where we want them. When they become overly concerned about their own salvation, they end up pursuing their "special" relationship with "god" and thus become more susceptible to us. They become so intent on their own salvation they never stop to think that the whole thing might be more about what our enemy desires than what the humans want.

I have used the fear of nonexistence or, worse, an eternity in torment for millennia to distract them and establish one of the most childish reasons for turning to "god." Fear of punishment and hope of reward has always been pretty thin gruel to sustain a relationship, even though, surprisingly, it has worked so well for us.

They become so fixated on whether they are going to heaven or hell, paradise or samsara, they forget all else in pursuit of this goal. As if it were really up to them anyway. They instinctually realize that something is wrong. They intuit that they don't live into a fullness that is available for them, but they can't quite put their finger on it. We can use this glimmer of recognition to pull them into an obsession with their own souls. How to restore their harmony or cast off bad karma becomes far more important to them than the suffering person next door. The flaw they know exists causes them to create their religions. Perhaps I will write more about religion in my next entry.

POSTED BY BLZBB AT 11:15 AM, 18/01
TAGS: HEAVEN | HELL | SHEOL | CHINVAT BRIDGE | MAYA

................................................................................

# Consider Job

Consider Job. I have always liked this story, if for no other reason than I have such a leading role. I especially enjoy the parts where I am able to goad "god" into bringing all manner of suffering, pain, and agony upon a devotee. I understand this—of course, it's kind of my trademark—but the fact that the story says "god" allows it? That just knocks me out every time I read it.

I also enjoy being portrayed as a prosecuting attorney. I do accuse them, all the time. I point the finger at them. I blame them. I accuse them to each other. I accuse them to themselves. *J'accuse!* It's what I do.

I love the justice aspect of this because I think the way that story gets told puts me in a rather positive light. I was only pointing out what seem to me to be perfectly good reasons for bringing them pain. I mean, seriously, how many of them really live up to their professions? Isn't their faith always contingent on the circumstances of their lives? I was only pointing out the obvious—as long as they have food in their bellies and someone to love, they will have faith. Empty their bellies, take away their loved ones, and they will howl at the moon with anguish. Even better is when they reject any notion that the universe actually cares about them.

So, when that story has "god" and me contesting for Job's body? I love the way that whole back-and-forth between us goes. I have so much power! I am particularly struck with the way that my arguments are so airtight they make "god" do my bidding. It was really a remarkable piece of work by whoever put that stylus to papyrus. I provoke *The Most High* into allowing pain, misery, and destruction to someone who was, and here I quote, "blameless."

How anyone could not become an atheist after reading the first two chapters of that book escapes me. Who would want to serve a "god" who allowed such pain and agony just to prove a point? I'll get into that whole issue another day, but for now I just want to point out some other things about this book I like so much.

I must admit, in its original form I liked it for all the above-stated reasons, but it is only when the other writers came along and put a little meat on the bones of the original story that it got really interesting. As I said, the first part of the story tells about how I talked "god" into letting me bring pain and suffering on the innocent. The victim, Job, didn't really protest, even though the missus herself told him to curse "god" and die. That is standard material right there. The righteous sufferer. Whatever.

But then those other guys come in and want to comfort Job. Man, I don't know who put that together, but they were freaking geniuses. Because what happens when the new writers come to the story is that they immediately get more honest about Job (and, by extension, themselves).

Once the action shifts, the first thing out of Job's mouth is "God damn the day I was born." It was a shriek of anguish, music to our ears. That always seemed like a more honest sentiment than "I came naked into the world, I'll leave it naked and it doesn't matter because 'god' is still blessed." What a load of crap that was. This other? This cursing of the Name? That I loved. I can't get enough of that. It was a simple and eloquent explosion of anger over his fate. I found it entirely appropriate considering the way that "god" treated him.

But what was even better were those friends. Whew, with friends like these, huh? I am sure they were sincere; in fact, the writer portrays them as sincerely believing the religious garbage they were throwing Job's way. But really, and this is one of my major points, it was pretty much religious ideology all down the line. This is the way it is with them; faced with pain on an unimaginable scale, they either become atheists, or they resort to this religion-as-a-projection ruse.

Take that first character in the story, Eliphaz the Te'manite (really awesome names, you must admit). He comes across concerned and caring, but when Job is at his lowest he says, and I'm paraphrasing here, "Yahweh punishes the wicked and rewards the righteous. You are being punished, so what sin have you committed?" How touching. We do like to kick someone when they are down, but *oy vey*!

The thing is, Eliphaz was only saying what humans have believed about their religions since the time they first became aware they were not the center of the universe. Retributive justice has been the air they breathe as far as religion goes. They are hardwired for it.

This has always been one of their foundational stories—"god" rewards the righteous and punishes the wicked. The idea undergirds everything they hold to be true and right. If they only knew. We have been able to use this idea in so many ways we don't want to disabuse them of the notion. They use this thought to keep the disorder from them. If they can convince themselves their salvation is in their own hands, they can ward off that fear of nothingness at the end. And, the thing is, this desire to control their fate shows up everywhere.

Consider the notion of karma, for instance. All things that happen to them are the result of their own actions. There is no innocent suffering. You have to hand it to them; they are relentlessly logical in working out how to keep the chaos at bay. What more logical scheme could you devise than one where every person's misfortune and suffering is a result of their own behavior? Even if you have to go back into another lifetime to make the argument, it is airtight; nothing can penetrate the logic of it. It is so well thought out there is not even the need for "god," just the ongoing energy of the universe.

Eliphaz and his buddies in their own way mirror this whole idea. They accuse Job of suffering because he has done something wrong. And the best part is that they have received this insight from "god." Yep, Yahweh's little helpers. Job ought to be happy to be undergoing this suffering because "god" cares enough to discipline him? How many times have we heard that around hospital beds?

Religion can be so much fun for us. Here this guy is at the edge of the precipice, and his friends come to offer some "comfort," while the whole time they are pushing him over the edge. I even heard a preacher in a hospital room say, "Oh, we're so sorry your baby has died. What sin did you commit that 'god' did this to you?" How can you not love it when abusing the victim comes cloaked in pastoral concern?

Of course, the other "comforters" are not much better. Well, maybe it wasn't Job but his children who sinned. Or maybe Job is just being obstinate and not owning up to what he has done. On and on it goes. The writers of this story are on to something. They were the original deconstructionists. But in this instance, Job's "friends" were using their religious ideology to crush another person. It's Job they want to demolish, not the ideology.

Job's buddies believe "god" doesn't punish a blameless man, because their ideology was, the righteous are rewarded and the wicked punished. Job keeps saying he didn't deserve this (and he's right, after all). Before too long, the whole thing turns into a pitched battle between Job and his "comforters," with Job holding onto his self-righteousness and his friends countering with their ideology.

This is why I like religion as ideology. The more we can keep it a belief system, locked into stiff and hidebound ways of understanding life, the better for our agenda. Religion builds a world that seems perfectly logical and appropriate to those who create it. This works to keep those fearful shadows that dance on the periphery of their minds at a distance. The fact that these things that they tell one another about how the universe works helps them to sleep at night and wake in the morning does us no real harm and, in fact, can be some of my happiest moments.

Like Job, they must all struggle at some point when that religious world of such careful construction starts to disintegrate under the assaults of everyday reality. When the wolf shows up at their door and takes his share and they sit on the ground with their head in their hands crying out, "But I didn't do anything wrong. I always went to services, I always sought to help the poor, I always did what my religion asked of me. Why me?" They cry to the universe and nothing responds to them. These are some of my fondest memories. You have to give it to them, it's a tough thing to work out, the whole suffering business, but they keep trying.

POSTED BY BLZBB AT 3:22 AM, 24/01

TAGS: JEWISH SCRIPTURE | HINDUISM | SAMSARA | RETRIBUTIVE JUSTICE | ÉMILE ZOLA | PETER BERGER, *THE SACRED CANOPY*

...................................................................................................

# Job Is Not Another Word for Work

Some of you are a bit dense. I want to write about other things, but you seem fixated on talking about religion. Let's return to Job for a minute. The reason why the writers of Job can be a little too insightful is that they realize on some level religion is mostly ideology.

Just the way they structure the dialogues between Job and his friends shows that these authors are closer to the truth than most. Notice, for example, that "god's" little helpers always seem to know exactly what "god" is thinking. Their arguments are full of "god" says this, "god" does that, on and on *ad nauseam*. But the gulf between them and the whole "god" business is so vast an uncharted territory they are lost at sea and have no idea how to reach shore.

Job's friends are blowing smoke. They have no idea why Job is suffering; they just don't want it happening to them. It makes *them* feel better to accuse Job because, if the righteous are rewarded and the wicked punished, they must be okay. Job is the one with the problem, not them.

These are the type of sentiments that deliver a thousand little wounds to the soul. They pick and pick at a person who is trying to maintain his integrity, until all but the strongest are ready to say, "Of course, you are right, I am wrong. Who am I to question the ways of the Most High?" And at that moment religion becomes the all-absorbing thing. This Most High must be appeased, perhaps by sacrifice, or if not that, then by surrender of the will. Are not sacrifice and suffering the noblest things in the world? Who could disagree with this? It's the backbone of religion.

What escapes their sight sometimes is how totalitarian and abstract this all is. If we can keep them focused on the All and Everything, we distract them from the one thing right in front of eyes. The One-All becomes a principle of life, not life itself, and everything must serve the principle, not the Life that nourishes the cosmos.

This should be pretty evident when we see how religion functions for so many of them. It's not like religion always leads people to freedom. It's more often the case that people become like Job's companions. Most people end up justifying themselves in the sufferings of others because they have internalized the ideology. As I mentioned previously, if "god" punishes the wicked and I am not suffering, it must only mean that "god" likes me and disapproves of the sufferer in front of me.

That is so cool because it kills two birds with one stone. (I love those quaint sayings they come up with sometimes, especially when it involves stones and dead things.) Their religion often leads them to self-righteousness and unconcern with the true suffering of another human being because they are trying so hard to justify themselves.

Now, as some of you mention, "god" does finally make an appearance in the story and, curiously, this is where the author tries to come to grips with the critique of religion and fails. Because when "god" makes an appearance in the story, "god" shuts up both Job and his friends. In the face of absolute power both parties must remain silent.

In the end, after all is said and done, they will go back to what they understand the most—power. It must have been difficult for the writers once they realized there was no way out of the hole they dug for themselves, no answer from the cosmos as to why they suffer so much.

After all the questions that have been raised about the way religion works to construct a world that isolates them from the suffering of one another, the only answer is that there is a vision of the "One" that is so overwhelming they must bow before it. Before, Job had heard of "god" with his ear, but now that they are face-to-face, Job capitulates. What kind of answer is that for all that has preceded the end of the story? But, in truth, what other answer could *they* have possibly given? Personally, I think "god" gets off too easy, because if you look at it from Job's point of view, "god" has a lot to answer for.

Of course, there is that whole tacking on of the story's original ending where Job gets all his stuff back, but this only points out how difficult it is to conceive of a universe where freedom comes in such costly ways. I like it when they never really pay any attention to all the stuff that goes on in the middle of the book. Most don't even know about all the struggles that happen in Job. It is much easier for them to just say, "See, Job was faithful in the midst of suffering, and in the end he got all his stuff back." You almost feel sorry for them and their willful ignorance, almost, but not quite.

POSTED BY BLZBB AT 8:59 AM, 24/01

TAGS: JOB | THEODICY | OMNIPOTENCE | ARCHIBALD MACLEISH, *JB*

# As Pure as the Driven Snow (If It Were in Beijing)

I want to pick up on something I touched on earlier about religion and the individual. It is true that the individual is important to our opponent, but in a different way than they are to us, or even themselves. And it is true that when some of the miserable creatures become aware that "god" loves them, and that something *is* at work in their lives, they do escape our grasp, though not our influence. This is where religion helps us.

Religion itself is just another path that they take to order their world. Religion has always been a way that they take aspects of their lives and implant them in transcendent reality. Religion is the one thing that allows them to root family, nation, culture, or tribe in a transcendent origin. Religion gives their lives a level of meaning that would otherwise be absent.

All the religious stories that they tell one another have the effect of legitimating their particular people through something beyond their world. "god," or whatever they want to call the thing, makes them special. They are the chosen, or the saved, or "the People." Whatever. The delusion is the same among them. They often take their own particular story and make it an absolute and universal one and then measure all other stories told against their own.

This is the part that we use so well because it leads to so much misery. They actually end up killing one another over whose story is best and true, or as one of them put it, whose imaginary friend is better. One of their storytellers, a Russian, caught this so well in his story of the Grand Inquisitor. He penetrated through all the absurdities of thinking that knowledge can ever be absolute. Because of their desire for the Absolute and the Universal they kill others whose "gods" are different and then demand that the vanquished worship the "gods" of the victors. But, even though this has been pointed out many times to them, they still persist in their folly. How can we not make use of this?

And this is just one little aspect of their religions that we can use for our purposes. There are so many more, so many ways we can distort an instinct in them they do not fully grasp. For example, we are able to take advantage of their idea of the Absolute. I find it amazing when they argue for moral absolutes, only to drop those supposed absolutes when it conflicts with their desires. Of course, murder is an Absolute when it comes to abortion, but when the time comes to send that child out to kill in the name of political or religious ideology, they have no problem sacrificing that life.

We can multiply these examples in numerous ways, but the result is the same. Those who define what constitutes a religious or even an ethical absolute will find things not as clear when it conflicts with what they desire. Evidently the Absolute for them means whatever they want it to mean depending on who they are and where they live. Everyone wants to see justice done to someone else.

This gap between the professed ideal and the lived life is part of the fabric of their lives, but the rank hypocrisy that emerges among the unreflective really warms my heart. They will scream and yell about some moral violation or the other, but turn right around and commit the same act themselves and not see the problem. For them, it's not even an issue. I sometimes think they were created more in our image then our enemy's. Don't you just love the way when they are thrusting a bayonet into an enemy's body they yell "Savage!" at their murdered foe?

This is one of those things that so annoyed me about the BODY. It was his willingness to relativize simply everything. Family, nation, society, even the law, were all relative to him. All the solidarities that tie them to something, all the things that we can use to manipulate people's feelings, he wanted to demote in favor of another realm, a world most unlike ours. Who can live in a world like that? Well, he could, I guess, but that just points out how hard a thing it is to live the way he did.

Just one more comment about this whole religion business for today. I also enjoy the feeling that their attachment to purity gives them. Have we not seen this all through their miserable existence? The desire for purity has created the conditions for countless slaughters. We have seen them bring the quest for purity into all aspects of their lives, but it often starts in their religious communities. They claim that "god" loves everyone, but *they* are really "god's" favorite. This means that all other people are actually not favored at all. You would think they would get that, but nope.

The marking of boundaries in this way all but ensures that others not of their community will have to suffer extermination. Look at their holy texts and see how this works itself out. Infidels, unbelievers, the unclean, the unsaved; all must be put out from the society because if they are allowed to live and flourish they will contaminate the true and pure.

Totalitarianism is never far behind the scenes in this, but they cannot for the life of them grasp that. You would have thought that the countless millions of Jews, Christians, Muslims, gypsies, ethnicities, and others served up for extermination would've taught them something. In the human's diseased mind, anyone who represented impurity should suffer extinction. Purity is an agenda for suffering and misery that takes even my breath away.

It is true that they have moved this dichotomy of the pure/impure to the political order now, but the religious order is still of use to us when we pull this string. The fact that they cannot themselves connect the dots from the killing of all those who were different in their sacred texts to Final Solutions only means that we will be able to play this hand until that great day when they erase themselves from the face of the earth. Child's play for us, as we have seen before. All we have to do is give them the material, and they will use it in ways that accomplish all our goals of pain, suffering, and death. This means more space for our desires to become manifest in their world.

POSTED BY BLZBB AT 10:19 PM, 30/01
TAGS: DOSTOEVSKY, *THE BROTHERS KARAMAZOV* | GENOCIDE

. . . . . . . . . . . . . . . . . . . . . . . . . . . . . . . . . . . . . . . . . . . . . . . . . . . . . . . . . . . . . . . . . . . . . . . . . . . . . . . . . . . . . . . . . . . . . . .

## New and Better Atheists, Please

Okay, I can see that the whole religion thing has excited many of you, given the comments you have made. I must say, though, colleagues, I am still curious where you get the idea that religion is an entirely harmful thing for the humans. I certainly did not mean to leave the impression that religion was all to the good for building our reign. No, religion has danger for us as well as for them.

First of all, not every religion is absolutely and totally an occasion for human ignorance. When you repeat the argument that all religion is good for us because of the violence and suffering it creates, you become the mirror image of those humans who argue that all religion is *bad* because of all the violence and suffering it brings.

It is more complex than this and makes me wonder if you have learned nothing. It is true that because of some of the things I have mentioned religion can be our great ally in spreading disillusionment and despair. The pure/impure tension works well for us, as does the self-righteousness that goes with it.

It is true as well that religion serves us when it functions as a projection of their wishes, hopes, and fears. We have trafficked greatly in religion as wish fulfillment. It is relatively easy to take their projections of what they hope for and lovingly fashion them into an agenda that becomes totalitarian and authoritarian.

Some of their thinkers and poets have seen this dynamic and pronounced, rightfully, how false and deceitful this makes religion. Who could not end up being disillusioned by their stupid crusades, pogroms, purges, and terrorism in the name of "god"? Religion has served us faithfully in this regard, and I anticipate that it will in the future.

When their "atheists" (how I love that word; it means nothing in the end) show how destructive religion is, it is just too easy. I really enjoy it when one of the believers is tarred with that brush. I had to hand it to that old bishop Polycarp back in the early years of Christianity. When the pagans had him in the Coliseum and the representatives of the empire told him he could live if he just denounced the atheists, Polycarp just looked around the Coliseum. The crowd was waiting for him to denounce his fellow believers, but he merely raised his hands to indicate the crowd in front of him and said, "Away with the atheists." Though that was the last thing he ever said, it took stones to do it. We could use people like him on our side.

The so-called atheists of today (not one of whom could hold Nietzsche's pen) who rail on about religion are pretty weak tea compared to those who really looked into the abyss and saw their reflections staring back at them. They knew the true consequences of their unbelief, the darkness, the despair that was inherent in their protests, and, in spite of it all, they leapt anyway. The leap of non-faith. I miss them.

How hard can it be today? Some thought they were on their way to eradicating religion and ushering in the new age of Enlightenment, where no "god" would command people's attention. Now we find a delightful resurgence of religion that can only help us in our ultimate goal. It is child's play to point to religious violence today. It exists on so many sides and is so prevalent that anyone can denounce religious violence and it just seems like common sense, not intellectual courage.

The present-day atheists think they are being brave and courageous for confronting the delusions of religion, but they become celebrities, famous figures who make good money stating the obvious to the simplest observer. They are extolled and celebrated, and for what? Religion is bad? What first-level idiot couldn't recognize that? Holy crap, it's enough to make you weep for Feuerbach and Nietzsche.

Really, those guys are hardly worth our time and are not much use to us. Some of them are as ideological as the most fundamentalist religious devotee. I'll have more to say about this later, but for now, I wonder why no one points out that politics has killed more people than religion could ever have imagined. Total up all the bodies that can be laid at the feet of their wars for power, and religion is a rank amateur in the death sweepstakes.

It is fun to watch people get all bent out of shape about the "suicide bombers" when they strap on their bombs and start rampaging. But talk about diminishing returns. Give me a nuclear bomb any day, dropped in the name of national pride and sovereignty. Take a moment, colleagues, and let that one marinate in your heads for a minute. Just think about the countless millions killed over the years in the name of social order. And the atheists think they are brave in denouncing religion? Let them try railing against democracy and see how far they get.

But would the celebrity atheists turn their critical thinking to this particular feature of human existence? Would they dare to be brave enough to turn their fire to the political orders that prevail on that planet today and try and penetrate the myths and narratives offered there?

The problem is that they still believe in things like democracy or socialism, liberty, freedom, and justice for all. Hell, they still believe that reason and rationality are something other than their own creation. They may be atheists, but they are still believers. Would they ask questions about the ideologies that demand the death of others who are different or who threaten their economic power? Would they make the connections that religion is used in the service of political orders that are far more powerful?

I certainly hope not, because if they did, the game might really be up for us. The type of discernment that would be able to penetrate the veil we have in place is not known among their atheists. (Well, there are a couple, but they are not listened to.) In his own way, Nietzsche understood the absurd truth of things, but no one really listens to him, do they? People are unable to see the truth he brought, and they just dismiss him as a bitter and crazy man. Well, he was that probably, but so much more.

Remember those stories when I had my interview in the desert with the BODY? I offered him all the kingdoms of the world in a moment of time and he refused. *He* may have refused, but since then it has been an unbroken stream of those who took me up on the offer. As we all know, once power has been taken, death inevitably follows.

What do you think would be the reaction if these atheists became true atheists? If they refused obeisance to all the "gods" created for them to worship? Can you imagine the reaction if the new atheists were to renounce the "gods" of nationalism, patriotism, capitalism, and commerce? What if they stopped worshiping the largest idol of them all, Reason?

What would be their reception if they became true prophets and called the entirety of the constructed world into question? Can you imagine they would get invitations to lecture at think tanks and universities? Do you think they would get hefty book sales if they were to make the connections between politics, order, and death? This might lead to questions about the ways that humans have arranged their entire societies, and we can't have that. I want them to embrace what they have built as what must be. They must never question their world in this way, and anyone who does must be silenced.

We should be glad they don't probe too deeply, colleagues. If they were to dig deeper, they would be too close to those we have most hated throughout time, like those Hebrew squawkers, the prophets. Those who acquire the vision to see things the way our opponent does threaten what we seek to construct. Even though many of them may not believe in our enemy, they are all the more dangerous to us because they are closer to something we detest—the Truth. And, if there is anything I hate it is the Truth. Sometimes I swear I hate it more than Love. I am the Father of Lies, not the truth.

I cannot write more today because right now I am too agitated. The thought of someone actually grasping the game makes me ill.

POSTED BY BLZBB AT 5:10 PM, 03/02
TAGS: CHRISTOPHER HITCHENS | RICHARD DAWKINS | POLYCARP, BISHOP OF SMYRNA | SIGMUND FREUD, *THE FUTURE OF AN ILLUSION*

# I'm Better Now, Thanks for Asking

Sorry I broke it off rather suddenly yesterday, but I had to go feed on something. The point I wanted to leave you with is that the present atheists are somewhat useful to us because, while they perceive the flaws with the forms and social manifestations of religion, they seem unable at this point to extend their critique to really grasp the deeper realities at play. As long as they feed people's disillusionment and create generations of mocking intelligentsia, we can use them. In this way they are of no danger to us, but not that much help, actually. I mean, we see little evidence that anyone listens to the intelligentsia anyway, bunch of elitists.

ME forbid though that they ever have the scales fall from their eyes and they see clearly. We don't care what they call the political or social orders that result in so much death; we are just happy when their love of self-destruction continues on without recognition or understanding of what they are doing. We want them to think in terms of their world as the *real* world. That way anyone who questions it can be dismissed as not living in the *real* world. Love your enemies? Not living in the *real* world. Forgive those who have wronged you? We don't do those kinds of things in the *real* world. You get the point, right?

But I also alluded in my last entry to the fact that some of you are not totally stupid. You recognize that religion is not absolutely bad. It does inspire some of them to lives that make us nervous. While we want to discredit religion we should not be deceived about the dangers that religion represents.

As much as it pains me to write what follows, we must not underestimate what we are up against. While we see how powerful a force religion can be for our purposes, it also has that property we detest. This is the aspect that creates the space for them to see the world and one another in new and different ways. Religion has enabled some of them to acquire a vision that sees further than I want them to see. It's like they see with their sight and "god's" sight at the same time. I. hate. this.

I despise it when they are able to see that love (ugh!) extends beyond the boundaries of their tribe, nation, or family. It means they no longer become defined by the order they are born into. It dawns on them that all these orders are not absolutes to be obeyed; they are constructions that are mostly contingent on history. This makes our work all the harder because we operate best when we can keep them separated from one another. The last thing I want is for them to see the deep interconnectedness that rests under all the diversity.

The worst moment for us is when they come to realize that our enemy pervades all existence and harm done to anything on the planet is harm done to the very thing that sustains their lives. This moves them into new territory and gives me anxiety. For us and our realm, everything depends on keeping this connection from them.

Once one of them comes to believe that "god" is intimately connected to life, immersed in it even, we lose another one of them for our work. They no longer want to kill in the name of the common good, they no longer act in ways that we can predict, and because we value control every bit as much as they do (where do you think they got their love of control from?), it should make us antsy.

POSTED BY BLZBB AT 11:29 AM, 04/02
TAGS: PANENTHEISM | AXIAL AGE | PROPHETS

# Control

As I mentioned upstairs, control is the driving engine of their violence, though they do not recognize it. Control of resources, control of capital, control of people, even control of nature—these are the dynamics built into their systems and is the spirit that in turn controls them.

We understand this because we love control. Control has always been dear to me and tops my agenda, my desires and hopes for them. I hope to tell you later how this works in matters like controlling bodies and even the consciences of those miserable creatures, because it is so much a part of their lives and is embedded in everything they do, from relationships to politics.

They mimic our desire to control by their use of propaganda to deceive and manipulate people. They count on the laziness of people not to think for themselves, not to reflect critically on the actions they are being asked to take, or the habits of thought they are encouraged to cultivate. They often don't think of what the ends of those things will be, while we know exactly where we want matters to end: in mushroom-shaped clouds rising thousands of times all over their planet, but more on that later.

In order to maintain control, they will enflame the masses with the cynical use of grievances and then profess surprise when the house goes up in flames, the body is at the end of the noose, and the corpses are stacked in a pile awaiting the fire. Though they can never quite articulate it, they will think that this is a small price to pay for the furtherance of their desire to control. Of course, this can never be called what it truly is; another name must be given for it. There have been many down through the centuries: divine right of kings, *pax Romana*, socialism, democracy, patriotism, and so on and so on . . .

POSTED BY BLZBB AT 8:23 PM, 05/02
TAGS: EMPIRE I REALPOLITIK I RUPERT MURDOCH I TABLOIDS

## Too Busy to Blog Today, but Stay Tuned

This will be a brief entry today as my attention is needed in maintaining our interests elsewhere. It appears that one of our theocracies is moving to strict repressions and our attention there must stay focused. Thanks to those of you who have written to express your concern, but I am sure with enough slaughter and blood we can bring things back into hand.

POSTED BY BLZBB AT 3:23 PM, 12/02
TAGS: THEOCRACY

## I'm Going to Disney World

I love Disney World. No, seriously, it is one of my most enjoyable places on the planet. It has given them so, so much: illusions, fantasy, Britney Spears. One small thing I have always enjoyed about it is the nuance and deception on display. Take Vegas, for instance. There we don't have to concern ourselves with working hard, the suckers come for pleasure, we give it to them (along with our requisite measure of pain), and while some of them go home happy, for most it is an empty experience. What happens in Vegas stays in Vegas, baby.

But Disney World is even better because we still fleece the rubes, but this time we use their most precious possession to do it, their children. Who can resist a child's plea for a *Little Mermaid* doll, or a *Lion King* game? They will spend as much money at Disney as at Vegas, but this time we can use children to extort the money, not showgirls. Either way, it's true what they say; a fool and his money are soon parted. How can we not love that?

POSTED BY BLZBB AT 1:00 AM, 13/02
TAGS: **BRITNEY SPEARS** | **BACKSTREET BOYS** | **MICKEY MOUSE**

............................................................................

## Play in Caesar's Ballpark, Play by Caesar's Rules

Back now to full-time blogging; thanks for your expressions of concern, but I think things went very well for us last week. We had to pay a lot of attention to the budding revolution seeking to make our theocracy accountable to the people, and I think for now terror and repression will buy us some time. I, obviously, was extraordinarily impressed with the speeches of their leaders: "Of course, we do not murder the protestors because we are evil. We take these measures of beating, burning, and repression with great sorrow in our hearts, even tears in our eyes."

Do you see how tragic and noble those words seem when uttered with such conviction of feeling? The depths of self-sacrifice come through when they say: "We are not doing this for our benefit, but for yours, and all those people who we will slaughter to maintain order will be on your heads, because you would not respond to our benevolence." I mean, really, that is such a transparent lie you have to wonder how they can even mouth such words with a straight face. The rhetoric of hell, Me bless them.

The beauty of it is that the oppressors are sometimes sincere in their belief. Do you see how the self-deception in the individual we discussed earlier blossoms into a wonderful bouquet of weeds? I mean, the hypocrisy of it is so obvious that even their comedians get it. Have you ever seen Monty Python's *Life of Brian*?

It is far more wonderful if we can attach the name of religion to political power grabs. As I have been contending, religion, when it is connected to the state, has always served our purpose of wholesale oppression. The dynamic is always the same, isn't it? Perhaps at first the religion itself is persecuted, but this just makes the believers more obstinate and they attract others by their courage and conviction. Over time (and, as we all know, it can take a very long time) the political order just exhausts itself trying to eradicate the faithful and eventually comes to realize that persecution is counterproductive.

We saw this plainly in the Christian religion. Given the revelation of the BODY, and of the Spirit's willingness to become embodied, to share their life, to actually become vulnerable to them, to suffer at their hands . . . well, you can see the problem we faced with this one.

And I have to hand it to them—those early Christians were, for the most part, pretty damn stubborn. For three centuries we did the best we could to marginalize them. We watched as the best pagan thinkers, the most respected of the culture, weighed in on how uncouth, how utterly naive, how truly dangerous to social order those superstitious believers were. Why, they didn't live in the *real* world.

The problem was that they gained ground on the *real* world every day. Even when the rulers went to empirewide persecutions, it just made things worse for our agenda. That is when we had our great insight: we were not going to beat them at our game (death, destruction, misery); we were going to have to try new tactics.

Thus, when the state declared a truce with them and stopped the repression, I was ready. After Constantine issued the toleration edict, no one worked harder than he to assimilate them. He saw the potential glue to hold the empire together was, in fact, the Christians. He was able to accommodate them and asked little from them—at first.

Put yourself in their position for just a minute. One moment you're being filleted and cooked on Rome's griddle, the next, Rome's emperor himself is paying for your representatives to come hang out and talk theology. Who wanted to go back into the desert of death Rome had been creating for three centuries?

So, slowly but surely, they put into place the means by which the inevitable compromises would take place. The law of love is replaced by the love of law (and, of course, order). If your religion is no longer being persecuted by the state, indeed, if the emperor himself has declared your religion the one that the empire will be built upon, you must start assuming some responsibility for what happens. Before allowing the Christians to wield power completely, the way was prepared by making them responsible for the empire.

How could they turn away? But with that responsibility so much else followed. For instance, doctrine emerged tangled up with political power, not necessarily the inner integrity of their revelation. Whatever truths there were to be found in their doctrines, it was always suspect if it could be changed depending on who had the emperor's ear.

It was no great surprise the rich wanted in on the action, so we saw some of the highest clerical offices go to those who were the most venal and corrupt, eventually right up to the pope. (Remember Formosus and Stephen VII? Good times!) I would like to say I saw it beforehand, but, actually, I didn't. The rapidity of their compromises took our breath away. Given the long arc of history,

I saw much success for our corporation in a very short period. The identity of the citizen became attached to a religion and a political order at the same time. It was brilliant, actually.

Once a person attaches their ultimate allegiance to a political order, they come deeper into our sphere. Say, for instance, your society is threatened by outsiders. In order to defeat the barbarian and save your people, deadly force must be necessary. "god" requires it. This thought permeates everything they think. No matter what society, I have observed the same thing over and over again. Slowly, but surely, where religion is present, the will of "god" becomes whatever the state says it is.

Do you remember when we had those wonderful scenes of Roman soldiers marching into tribal encampments in Germany and lining up people at the edge of the river and having the priests come along and baptize them? Walking among them, sprinkling water and invoking the Threesome, and pronouncing them Christian. As if this were all it took to become a follower of the BODY.

They thought they could actually convert people that way. Can't. Stop. Laughing. Making the mistake of thinking that Spirit works from the outside in, they sought to "Christianize" the world. Think of all the good this did for our realm in the following years. I'm just glad they kept the pagan worship of trees as a custom. I've always liked green; it's one of my favorite colors. It sets off red so well.

They made a large move toward us when they started to justify war in the name of "god." The first arguments of this were how to save society and protect the innocent from the "barbarians." The rules were very prescribed, and great care and thought was taken for how to channel human aggression. But how quick a step from just war to holy war we saw. They moved rapidly from wars to protect the innocent, to wars for empire or, better, wars against heresy. I could not have imagined in my wildest dreams they would depart from the teachings of the BODY so quickly.

Though, I suppose, I shouldn't have been so astonished. This move to legitimate their religion brought both their undying idealism and their never-ending optimism into our arena, and once you play in Caesar's ballpark, you play by Caesar's rules. Good for us. I may have more to say about this later, but for now I have other matters to attend to. Someone wants to burn a witch in Bulgaria. Fabulous!!

POSTED BY BLZBB AT 4:02 AM, 16/02

TAGS: CONSTANTINE I EDICT OF MILAN I ROMAN EMPIRE I COUNCIL OF NICAEA I *O TANNENBAUM* I ALEXANDER VI I JUST WAR I CRUSADES I ENVY

. . . . . . . . . . . . . . . . . . . . . . . . . . . . . . . . . . . . . . . . . . . . . . . . . . . . . . . . . . . . . . . . . . . . . . . . . . . . . . .

# Religion(s)

One thing we can count on with humans is that they seek to systematize everything. This is a propensity we have observed that does delight us. Their lives need to be negotiated among the variety of traditions they establish, but often this is too complicated for them, so they will work to take all the diversities and shove them into a narrow tube to better digest things. Talk about sausage making.

The joy of this is not lost on us, is it? Personally, I am pleased when they are uncomfortable with the differences in their lives. I appreciate that there are those who contend for only one true Christianity, one Judaism, one Islam, one Hinduism (although, let's face it, with monism the heavy lifting has been done already). The diversity of contexts, cultures, and people who inhabit and shape those traditions can become obscured over the fight that often breaks out among them over whose version is the "right" one.

It is more difficult for them to think that there are different forms of Christianity, Islam, Judaism, or any other religion. It is hard for them to negotiate among their differences and grasp the underlying possibility that in all this diversity they are connected to our opponent.

Many of them cannot find a home in the differences of their own traditions, never mind those other ones. Uncomfortable, they struggle with those who should be companions on the journey and turn them into enemies. It's Protestant against Catholic, Sunni against Shiite, and us against them all. In the meantime, our realm grows.

Even their texts reflect the diversity, but this makes them anxious as well. They try to take all the tensions inherent in their sacred texts, the variety of images of "god," and systematically control the message. Eventually they seek to control "god" as well.

Good things happen for our firm when their humanly constructed ideas are offered up as absolute truths, and others are forced to bow the knee or die. You would think after centuries of this foolishness they would wise up, but, fortunately for us, they never do. Although, come to think of it, they are making a tad bit of progress in this area; we just have to make sure it never mainstreams.

The challenge of the present for them will be negotiating how to live among this diversity and fragmentation. They must make their homes in this incoherence to some extent, but the possibilities in this diversity are not seen by most of them. They remain uncomfortable in their ambiguity, and we welcome the possibility that the new dark age is upon them and they do not grasp it. Who said the crusades were a thing of the past?

We now don't have to rely on the hegemony of the one true story to force them into line; we have the tyranny of a thousand narratives to carry out our work. We now have the tribes arrayed against the global collective, and this suits me, for they still seem unable to create the type of communities where the spaces exist for their differences to inform and enrich their traditions. From our perspective, it is as satisfying to watch Muslims kill one another in Darfur or Christians kill one another in Ireland as it is to watch Christians kill Muslims or Hindus kill Sikhs. Either way, as I said before, we build our world, the *real* world.

POSTED BY BLZBB AT 3:59 AM, 17/02
TAGS: **PARLIAMENT OF THE WORLD'S RELIGIONS** | **PLURALISM** | **NORTHERN IRELAND** | **IRAQ** | **JERUSALEM**

.........................................................................................................

# Hammer, Meet Nail

I sometimes don't know why you are all so dense. In response to my ongoing vision statements, some of you were confused as to why we had to bother with subtlety or stealth. "Why not just go full bore and stop worrying about the nuances?" one of you asked. Really? Sometimes you sound much like them. The least effective of them are full of bluster and bravado about what they would do if put in situations that demanded courage and action. It's easy to stumble into action, especially when you don't carefully consider the consequences. They rarely consider the necessity for wisdom, but we should at least be wiser than they are.

Some of them, of course, are consistent in arguing for a blunt-instrument approach for everything. These types have always been readily available to us. We give them the hammers and everything looks like nails. So, they smash their world up in the name of their ideologies, personal slights, and hatreds. I especially enjoy it when they work to demonize those with whom they disagree.

These have always been our useful fools, and they are dependable because we can count on them to never, ever deviate from their hidebound ways. They howl for action and force. "Something must be done!" they scream. One of the reasons this is so helpful to us is that in their blundering stupidity, they forget that it is usually the case that they caused the situation at hand.

How many times have we watched them engage in some action with the purpose of "promoting liberty" or "protecting freedom" or even "serving God" when they had not even thought to question whether their much-loved freedom, liberty, and obedience had died at their hands? They have absolutely no sense of the long-term consequences.

Once their rhetoric has achieved a certain status, they no longer control it—it controls them. Thus, they are compelled to repeat the same mistakes over and over again. They arm those fighting their enemy and then seem surprised when their enemy sends them terrorists in return. We don't care who wins because as long as there is death we are able to feed. What was it one of their authors said about "Death Eaters"? I'm just glad most of them don't know how close she was to the truth.

But, you see the point? We find it easier to use those who are unable to temper their passions. Even if their passions are aroused toward something that is ostensibly worthy and noble, the very fact that they are taken captive by their ideology means they have grown a handle we can grip. More often than not they are unaware of how deeply they are shaped by conditions that are so transitory. Seriously, how often in the historical stream of things does anything remain permanent? Today's empire becomes tomorrow's history lesson.

They will kill in the name of the fatherland, the homeland, even heaven or paradise without a second thought. Their blather about how strong they are is rather pathetic because they fail to see what real strength looks like. They become defined by their enemies, thereby becoming weak, and then they are in much greater danger because their enemy enters them in a way they do not even begin to grasp.

This is why we use the methods that we use. We must not for a minute think of allowing our enemy the ability to enter us. We must be strong and resolute in the face of the One who oppresses us. We must police ourselves and give no ground for any of our opponent's strategies. Otherwise, we will end up looking like appeasers, and we hate that.

And we must, above all, instill this spirit in those whom we can use to bring death and destruction. No compromise, no quarter given, evil must be met head-on and resisted to the death. (We love the resistance-to-the-death part the best; so very noble, so very tragic.) That's the way the *real* world works, isn't it?

If they realized that evil met head-on is one of our greatest goals, they would change their tune, but they don't know how things really work. Meeting evil head-on puts them on our ground and, once there, we will always win. This is how we want them to think. We don't want them to consider how resistance to evil early on would snuff out the flame we seek to fan. What would Germany (or the rest of Europe for that matter) have looked like if its citizens had refused to hate the Jews? True resistance to evil never comes from weapons; it comes from a heart that refuses evil's call to hate, or fear. By the time they get to guns and knives it is too late for them. They are already in our hands.

The ones that really bother me are the ones that don't become obsessed with eradicating evil. They don't become fixated on the evil of those they oppose to the point that we can use them so broadly. There are those who recognize the evil in a particular situation, take it seriously even, but they don't allow us to absorb them. They move by other means to blunt our impact and keep us from the space that is rightfully ours.

When the BODY showed up, well, that scared the hell out of me, I must say. He understood that the *real* world is, in fact, an illusion that they grasp like dying persons holding onto life. I am not surprised they wanted to kill him. They realized what a threat his way was to true evil. If they lived like the BODY desired, we could not exist. *I* could not exist.

POSTED BY BLZBB AT 6:47 AM, 18/02
TAGS: NEOCONS | J. K. ROWLING | INCARNATION | SERMON ON THE MOUNT

. . . . . . . . . . . . . . . . . . . . . . . . . . . . . . . . . . . . . . . . . . . . . . . . . . . . . . . . . . . . . . . . . . . . . . . . . . . . . . . . .

## Resistance Really Is Futile

As I wrote earlier, it is always best for our side if we can convince them that whatever evil they face must be met with extreme prejudice. We must make sure they do not recognize the power of indirection and nuance. If they demonize something hard enough, they lose sight of the fact that the same thing is in them. We want them to tap into their hate by their very struggle with what they have defined as evil.

In this way we are able to establish our influence. We colonize them with all manner of behavior, and it is only later, after the fog of war or anger has lifted, that they ask themselves how they could have acted that way. This blindness helps us in so many ways.

First of all, it appeals to their ever-present self-righteousness. There has never been a time when any nation, tribe, family, or individual saw themselves on the *bad* side of things. When they have convinced themselves their enemy is the very embodiment of evil, they will unleash mindless violence and destruction upon one another.

"Remember," they tell themselves, "we are only killing so that we can make the world a safer place." Before too long, no one really remembers what happened to kick the killing off. They just keep focusing on the injustices done to them as they are killing all their enemies. They never remember the killing they did or the reasons for why they have enemies in the first place.

This has been one of the best things about memory we have been able to distort. They take their memories and turn them to the hurt and wrong done to them, and those injustices will sit like a smoldering fire for *centuries*. This brings me great joy. The suffering that I so appreciate has a built-in mechanism for continuation. It is like a self-perpetuating machine. Who could not love that?

The best part is that there *are* real injustices, real horrors that they do to one another, but they have no idea how to break the cycle themselves. So, they wait for some moment of transgression in time and then all the past is called up as if time collapsed and five hundred years ago were yesterday (our little twist on the whole "a day is as a thousand years in 'god's' sight" thing). Then it's guns and knives, pitchforks and bombs. If some of you doubt my analysis so far, I have just one word for you—Balkans.

You can see the brutal efficiency of this. It has been the fuel that ignites a thousand fires of destruction and lights a million tiny flames of bitterness and hate. It has given us our best results for the ultimate goal toward which we are working. All these endless permutations of slaughter and death, justified in the name of the good and just. One of the slight beauties (yes, we have our own notion of the aesthetic) of this is that they are in charge of their own fate. This is all done by their own hands. As much as I want to take credit, the devil did not make them do it.

They continue the killing in the name of their *real* world. "We must do these things because the world is full of dangerous and evil people who must be stopped before they can kill us." The beauty of this is that the same human memory that recalls with exquisite detail the harm done to its tribe a millennium ago is unable to accept responsibility for the evil they visited on another community just the other day. Those precious fools are their own stand-up routine.

This is where Nietzsche was so clever, because he saw through their deceptions and obfuscations and just told the truth. He may have provided an antidote for what ailed them, but not the cure. Sometimes he could be a little too insightful. He could even make me a bit nervous. He once wrote, " 'I have done that,' says my memory, 'I cannot not have done that,' says my pride, and remains inexorable. Eventually memory yields." Though Nietzsche wasn't talking about marriage, we have seen this dynamic work there as well. As I said before, they don't even know their own capability for self-deception. I just hope they don't ever see that clearly how they distort their lives.

It excites me to see this in them. I cannot for the life of me figure out why our rival allows them to develop in this way. Wouldn't it be better just to exterminate them, the way we want to, and start over again? It's not like that isn't a plotline that transcends all their particular religious stories. Death, Destruction, New Creation, Shiva, Vishnu, Kali, the Rider on the White Horse, Apollyon the destroyer—all these appear in their narratives. No one has a monopoly on destruction.

But I am getting a little off my main point. They create their own reality because of their inability to grasp the true nature of things. There are a million ways they do this, but to us it ultimately leads to the same place—their continued and premature deaths.

They convince themselves violence is the only way they can resist evil. Those who have some idea of how our opponent works are almost always ostracized and marginalized when they point out there is a better way of resolving and reconciling their conflicts. Usually those who think themselves the strong ones mock those who disagree. Those who think they live in the *real* world consider all those who live in our opponent's world weak.

But where is real strength to be found, colleagues? Is it in those who are manipulated by their enemies into actions that ensure the narratives of injustice can continue? Or is true strength found in those who are able to generate the type of memories that create new and different worlds? If they only knew how much we fear those who offer true insight. This is why we work so hard to make the truly wise among them appear to the world as irrelevant or subversive of the "necessary" orders humans have built.

Sometimes we find that those few souls who have the discipline to live differently attract attention. Then we just convince the rest of them they don't have that strength. "You can admire this, but you are not capable of it." So, for every Nelson Mandela, Dalai Lama, or Dorothy Day, for every Oscar Romero or Aung San Suu Kyi (and let's be clear, they themselves are not without their faults) who resists oppression with grace, or bloodlust with forgiveness, there are millions who feel unworthy of such feats.

Of course, we are able to make *our* exemplars so much more powerful than those who serve the cause of agape. I am thinking here of the painter from Austria with the funny mustache. The fact that he continues to serve us still even after his death is icing on the cake.

POSTED BY BLZBB AT 3:56 PM, 20/02

TAGS: ESCHATON | NELSON MANDELA | DOROTHY DAY | OSCAR ROMERO | DIETRICH BONHOEFFER | STAR TREK | THE BORG | ADOLF HITLER | MIROSLAV VOLF, *EXCLUSION AND EMBRACE*

## Memories May Be Beautiful and Yet, What's Too Painful to Remember We Simply Choose to Forget

I read somewhere recently that when the question was raised how many Serbs were killed in Croatian concentration camps during the Second World War, Serb historians came up with the figure of 700,000 victims. Curiously enough, when Croatian historians looked at the same question, they came up with the "fact" that "only" 30,000 Serbs were killed.

Funny thing, memory. As I said above, it not only remembers what "was," it also remembers what "should" be in the future. It is another fine testimony to our rule that memory will construct the future justifications for slaughter in order to hide present guilt. How often does memory actually recall events the way they "really" were? Or, is it the case that memory creates the cloak of justification for what is to come?

I have often spoken of the regime of the lie and the regime of the truth. Where do you think those come from? Who establishes the truth among them? It is those who control the power of memory. If this power rests with the Mullahs and clerics, they establish the truth; if it rests with politicians, they establish the truth; if it rests with scientists, they do. We don't care who has the power to decide; we only want them to stay blind to the truth our enemy seeks to reveal to them.

Truth is created by power, and memory contains far more power than humans realize. Memory can mobilize a country to genocide. As long as they remain unaware of how this works, I foresee many possibilities for our gaining ground. Devotion to the truth can serve many masters, but we have often seen how truth for them is the club they use to beat others into submission.

POSTED BY BLZBB AT 12:45 AM, 21/02

TAGS: RWANDA | SERBIA | CROATIA | BARBRA STREISAND, *THE WAY WE WERE*

## Hitler Was Not That Special

In a previous entry, I mentioned my servant Adolf, but some of you were so dense you could not figure out what I was getting at. Sometimes you are dumber than Jesus' disciples. Seriously, have you read how stupid they could be at times? *Duh*-sciples is more like it. Yes, Adolf served us well with his slaughter in the name of purity. A virtuoso of will and malignancy if ever there was one. But he helps us still because he has become a fetish, a symbol invoked by the humans to justify their fight against evil. In just this way they do not recognize that Hitler was as human as they.

Think of all the times Hitler is invoked when they use him as shorthand against one another. They don't care that they are being lazy and stupid; they never do. They just throw the word out there and think that will shut down all conversation about the courses of action and motives of their opponents.

That is amusing, but one of the best parts is when Hitler becomes shorthand for "Absolute Evil." This allows us to cloak ourselves far more invisibly. They refuse to accept the fact that their actions serve us because they do not rise to the level of Hitler's type of malevolence. "Well, at least I'm not killing ten million people," they argue, as if the scale of their crimes has anything to do with moral equivalence.

Even the dimmest of you can see the sheer magnificence of this. We can take the impulse for self-preservation they possess and twist that to a point where they willingly violate everything they hold dear in the name of the good. As long as they call that good "security" or "protecting the _____ way of life" (just pick a country and fill in the blank, it's all the same to us.), we find that space to live we are looking for.

They will not recognize that they are becoming the thing they fear. And they most certainly do not realize they are replicating what Hitler brought to us and laid at our feet. Yes, perhaps they do operate on a much smaller scale. We are presently working on the scale issue though, which was much improved in the last century when they discovered the power of the atom. That opened up more possibilities than we could ever have imagined. This is something I will talk about later because it is our great secret, and I see that they love the secret. But my main point is that we are able to colonize them when they resist their opponents with such force.

For instance, take torture. This has always been one of our most effective weapons. We have taken great pride in their ingenuity when giving their fellow human beings more pain and suffering than the victims imagined possible. And the creativity . . . who would have thought they would have such a talent for inflicting pain? Someone was promoted when they realized humans only too readily would take up demonic behavior.

Torture is one of those things that we love because it creates its own descent into madness. Once begun, if the person involved doesn't stop immediately, their soul becomes more closely aligned to ours. In the beginning it is always necessary, they tell themselves. *How else will we get this woman to confess she's a witch unless we make her?* And as they proceed, what poor wretched creature wouldn't confess that they had coupled with me if only to spare their lives a bit more pain before they are put to death?

Ah, the sheer glory. With torture, a person can be made to say anything that accords with what the torturer actually believes is going on. They delude themselves by saying that they must protect the village from witches. In order to do that they must find out who the witches are. When they torture, they find that the witches were really there all along, and now that they have confessed they can put the poor creatures out of their misery and protect the village. Humans love to find scapegoats to release their violence and destruction on, saving themselves from turning those energies on one another. Torture has always been one of the most effective arrows in our quiver.

Dear tast—um, tender colleagues, take that propensity in them and extrapolate throughout history. Only now take something they actually know is there, say, terrorists, and do the same thing. Whisper it in their ear. Have in mind what you want from the terrorist, torture him enough to verify your perspective, and you get instant justification for whatever it is you want to do. It is foolproof in a way. You can create any reality you want under these conditions. But the true evil of it is hidden from all except those in the room.

Oh, at first you can play on the torturer's sense of right, wrong, patriotism, or tribalism—whatever it takes. But soon enough they are so open to us they fall faster and faster, to the point where the first delicious feeling of enjoyment sweeps over them. They can still think of themselves as good people. They are only following orders. But deep down in the spaces of their psyche, where no one else sees, they begin to look forward to the whimpers, the screams, the cries of, "Please, no more; I'm a human being." Not to the one with the paddles and the electricity and the water, they're not. To them, the tortured are just the enemy. And, now, the enemy is in their hands and at their mercy. You see how this replicates life in hell? Control, obedience, loss of soul equals more space for us to stretch out in. Ah, torture, a foretaste of things to come.

This type of power over the body of another is absolutely intoxicating. I remember so well that power when we had the BODY. This is a power that has seduced countless numbers of them over the millennia, the power to control life itself. They actually begin to love their work. There are no hesitations, no concerns about what is happening to their soul, because they are "saving the world."

As an aside, I must confess, when we planted that idea about moving the justification for torture into their entertainment venues, thus pushing it out from darkened rooms and shadowy spaces, I never imagined we would be so successful. I still can't believe how many of them saw nothing wrong with torture as long as it "saves lives." I never in my wildest imagination thought the so-called bomb-going-off-any-minute scenario would actually become a factor in their decisions. This is just another reason why I love them so. They give themselves to us so easily.

They also don't suspect the damage it does to the soul of their societies. If we can get them to waterboard some deluded fool 183 times, we have moved them beyond the usual transgressions into territory from which it is hard to come back. And, colleagues, we must keep this from them; because torture all but guarantees that the cycle of revenge and death we enjoy so much will continue.

I especially love the violence of it. The pain they administer to one another becomes so intense that the gift of language is taken from them and they are reduced to inchoate rages against the dying of the light. The screams of the tortured are like our version of speaking in tongues, but instead of a heavenly language, they shout the language we build our world around. It is the language of anguish, suffering, and bewilderment that humans could do this to one another. Yes, these are a few of my favorite things.

POSTED BY BLZBB AT 9:21 PM, 21/02

TAGS: RENDITION | ABU GHRAIB | JACK BAUER

# Between the Inquisition and the Gulag

I have so enjoyed reading your comments on my last post and want to take a minute to respond to them. First of all, thanks to all of you who sent in reports of your progress in the area of "enhanced interrogation techniques." It is gratifying to see something so horrific, something that is such a violation of human dignity, acquiring such commonplace justification that their most powerful leaders can legitimate the worst murders and the sheep silently accept it. No war crimes, no tribunals, no justice. Just the arguments about why these "behaviors" are legal and hence justified. We have a special place waiting for the architects of that policy.

This is why the law has always been so useful to us. Of course I hate it when society has common consent and community involvement in the creation of the law. Then everyone believes they are subject to the rules because everyone agreed to them. From the most powerful to the least, they all see themselves as responsible to one another, and the law they create brings them a sense of community as well as order. Generally we like order—a *lot* of it, actually. But when they enter into order freely, without coercion, we are most displeased.

Fortunately, over the years we have been able to disabuse them of the notion that anything like a moral universe undergirds the laws they create. They have done a good job of legitimating their social orders on the basis of laws they created, but we have also been very successful in twisting these to our liking.

In our best cases, the law becomes what the powerful of society say it is, and, as said before, they will wield this like a club to beat others into compliance. The rules then become distorted, creating certain habits that will eventually poison their society. If the laws do not protect the weak and powerless, but privilege only those who have access to the creation of them, we have fruitful ground to work.

They have mostly discarded the notion that something like a moral universe exists. Even if they keep the notion, believing that their creations have some innate connection to that morality, they still end up building something much to our liking. They actually think they can recognize the difference between right and wrong. Better yet, they actually think their ideas of right and wrong are the same as our opponent's. When they cling to their law, believing it to be "god's," we are pleased. How much suffering has entered into their lives by those determined to impose "god's" law on the world? But I digress.

I really wanted to write some more about torture. It makes me happy. And, as stated before, it makes me especially happy to see the "civilized" nations of the world using it so much these days. Torture in their minds is a search for the Truth, but in reality it is the regime of the Lie they find there. This should tell them something about their self-deception, but fortunately they are too blind to grasp the truth of the thing. They convince themselves they are after the Truth, but it is the regime of power that truly captures their attention.

I alluded earlier to the way that sometimes torturers become deluded when they believe *they* are suffering because they are willing to enter the darkness for the sake of their society. You can see this in the sincere expressions of their leaders when they sadly proclaim in public forums that they have to work in the "shadows" in order that people might have lives full of sunlight. We could not do a better job of reframing evil in the name of good.

But what would happen if the sunlight were to fall on those shadows? Would it give the lie to what is really taking place? It would be a most unwelcome outcome for us, to be sure. We would miss the small brutalities, the larger violations, and the deaths, because these things serve our cause. But we can rest assured that this seldom happens, because people so value their lives they are willing to justify any slaughter deemed necessary to save them. What will it profit a person to gain "security" but lose her soul? A place at our table, to be sure.

What gives us greater amusement, however, is what happens when it comes to light that some other society is using torture. The torturers become very self-righteous about how torture is barbaric (demonic is more like it), and how all the information given under torture by others must be lies because they were coerced. Shrieks of laughter in hell follow, don't they?

At the same time that politicians are denouncing the sight of some pathetic broken thing in another country "confessing" to crimes against the state, they use the information they get from their own torture to justify wars that will destroy the worlds of countless people. All of this is done in the name of the good, of protection and security, of the *real* world, of course. Every day they embrace our logic a bit closer to their hearts.

They justify this by arguing their torture is different from the others. Their torture must be done because the enemy they face is inhuman and will not own up to the evil they are doing. This torture is just seeking to save lives and ensure the public order. Those others who are torturing are trying to control free men and women.

In the end it is all the same—torture establishes the power of the state over the individual. By attacking the individual body, however, the state attacks its own body and does not even recognize the damage it does to itself. Eventually, the degeneration and rot will set in, and events will move them in our direction. We have brought down so many to our level by these actions. History itself bears witness to our effectiveness.

POSTED BY BLZBB AT 10:03 PM, 27/02

TAGS: GUANTANAMO | INQUISITION | EL SALVADOR | CHILE | ARGENTINA | ALEKSANDR SOLZHENITSYN | WILLIAM CAVANAUGH, *TORTURE AND EUCHARIST*

........................................................................................................

# Revelation

My mentioning the Rider on the White Horse a couple of entries ago confused some of you, so I thought I would take a minute to address that. One of you asked if I was referring to Clint Eastwood. Really? You must be new around here. I know we work hard to make any kind of real familiarity with sacred texts unknown to those in love with modernity, but I never dreamed we were this successful. Eastwood was the Pale Rider.

Nope, the image I was referencing comes out of a book that I personally have a love-hate affair with, the Revelation to John. Not so heavy on marketing to be sure, but still, it has stood the test of time. The reason I hate this book is because it says we lose in the end. The writer wants to make that point, drive it home, and the best way of doing this is to portray a narrative where in the end good triumphs over evil. Well, we'll see about that, won't we?

Of course, when the book was being written the followers of the BODY were having a terrible time of it, which was to our liking. The book was meant to encourage them that good would triumph over evil. Why is that such a compelling story line for humans?

The reason I love this book is that it has endlessly amused me for centuries. I was almost disappointed when they came close to not putting it into their Scriptures, but they finally came around. Good for us they found it useful. Since that time, Revelation has been, on balance, more useful for us than it has for those it was originally intended.

I especially enjoy the way they interpret the symbols and images in the book with whatever pops up in the fertile fields of their imaginations. Through the years, they have devised some of the most inventive and hilarious interpretations of that text. They have done things with that text that we ourselves could not have imagined. I am truly in awe of their creative powers sometimes. It actually makes me a tad jealous.

There have been numerous occasions through the centuries when they head to the hills or out to the desert to await the return of the BODY. They pore over the pages of the text incessantly, thinking the end of the world is near. Of course, when the end of the world doesn't come, then they have to devote their energies to making something up about why the event didn't take place when they thought it would. How sweet is that? Not only do they discredit themselves, but they also ensure that no one in their right mind takes this book seriously.

Some of them take special delight in the belief that when the BODY returns he's going to be really pissed. We're talking genocidal, mass-killing, holy-terror, earth-shattering pissed about all the suffering his followers have had to endure. The thought never occurs to these people (many of whom won't be happy in heaven unless they know someone else is in hell) that the whole purpose of the book was to comfort those who suffered persecution and that their oppression would end.

Typical of the humans, those who read Revelation in any age think it was written for their time. In every generation's preoccupation with themselves, this book has always been about them. They are at the center of "god's" plan for the last days. The irony is that the book *is* about them; just not in the way they think it is.

POSTED BY BLZBB AT 1:12 AM, 01/03

TAGS: NERO | ROMAN EMPIRE | APOCALYPTIC LITERATURE

.....................................................................................................

# Getting Our Apocalypse On

I remember once there was this group of fanatics back in the sixteenth century that took over a German town, Münster. Those in the grip of that particular madness threw out all the Catholics and Protestants and instituted a reign of holy terror and insanity. It was glorious what took place there.

What a parade of weird that was. And the best part? This was all due to the influence the book of Revelation had on their imaginations. They were running through the streets naked at night, proclaiming the day of the Lord was at hand, taking hot pokers to their mouths, and all in the name of a soon-returning king. Ah, good times! In the end, after the powers outside the gates closed the city off from the outside, they ended up eating rats, dogs, and other things so vile it made even us a bit queasy, though some of that was from laughing so hard. An entire community unraveling, and the beauty of it all, the piece that fascinated us? This debacle was supposed to be the New Jerusalem being prepared for the return of the BODY. Now, where do you suppose they got an idea like that?

It has been this way for hundreds of years. People read Revelation and make assumptions that theirs is the time when it all happens. They think they stand at the end of time and slip over the falls of lunacy like people used to do in barrels over Niagara Falls. I like my buckets full of crazy, but the ones that have floated over the cliffs of apocalypticism have just been precious to us.

You would think they would learn over the years to temper this thing, to maybe consider that Revelation is not necessarily a blueprint for the future, but no, it just gets better and better. Even in the modern world we have those out there who become so enamored of Revelation they just cannot help themselves. They spend their entire lives waiting for the BODY, but he never arrives. At least not the way they were expecting.

Some of them make a fortune out of peddling story lines based on the fantasies they have devised in their heads, but it seems like such a small reward for the work they are doing. When their world leaders start speculating about whether prophecy is coming true, we rejoice. They become so obsessed with the return of the BODY they usually don't put much thought into how they should live in the present. That works for us, actually.

Even in Jerusalem we see the impact of Revelation when one of the really nutty ones gets it into their mind that they must blow up the Dome of the Rock in order to ensure that Jesus returns. Talk about "god's" little helpers. Like "god" needs C4, huh? Have they ever taken a close look at interstellar space? Explosions all over the place out there.

These believers are all sincere. That is part of the beauty. Question them on their interpretations and they look at you earnest and heartfelt and say yes, this is the way the world comes to an end. They live in a unique time, unlike any other time in the world, and this will be the moment that the BODY comes back. Like they knew. You keep expecting the little wink, the subtle smile to play out on their lips, the shake of the head to indicate that they know what they are doing, but no such thing.

They don't realize they are creating a false consciousness that dominates millions of people's lives. They plant the seeds, and those seeds continue to grow with each succeeding generation. The

Scofield Bible leads to *The Late Great Planet Earth,* which in turn generates *Left Behind* books. Good for us. We love it when they spend all their time speculating on when the BODY returns. We find it absolutely astonishing that they will invest so much energy in obsessing over the "signs of the times." (I hear, for instance, that there is a computer in Brussels that bears one of my names, The Beast. I bet you didn't know that, huh?)

Those captivated by Revelation seldom contemplate what the world would be if their lives were lived the way our opponent wishes. It never occurs to them that the BODY returns when they live truthful lives, lives without deception. It escapes them that the BODY returns every time one of them lives into his vision of what humanity should be. Every moment love is chosen instead of hate, peace instead of war, reconciliation instead of revenge, is a moment that the life of "god" becomes embodied in the world. I detest this; it goes completely against my goal of full-spectrum dominance.

As long as they remain in their deceptions and focus on riders on white horses, beasts from the sea, and whores, we can fill the empty spaces with ideas to our liking and keep them from considering that every day they themselves have responsibility for the return of the BODY. If they want to think the return happens because things blow up, well, more power to them I say.

POSTED BY BLZBB AT 9:23 PM, 02/03

TAGS: HAL LINDSEY | TIM LAHAYE AND JERRY JENKINS | J. N. DARBY | PLYMOUTH BRETHREN | DISPENSATIONALISM | C. I. SCOFIELD | C4

........................................................................................

## Don't Hate the Playa, Hate the Game

Now, hear my accusation—why does "god" get to establish "god's" realm in utter and absolute violence and we do not? Why does "god" get to destroy the world and we do not? Why does "god" get the power to say, "I am the Almighty, I have become the destroyer of worlds," or something to that effect? Religion cannot exist without that cry.

Think of the stories where everything is swept away by a flood or fire of divine retribution with only a remnant being spared. How could divine judgment fall on someone like Hitler, or Robespierre, or on us, for that matter, without the accusation being hurled back: "But, we learned it from you. We saw that if the earth is to be made pure, if evil is to be destroyed, if the great crimes of the rich and powerful, the masters, are to be met with justice, then all must be erased. All must perish before our righteous quest must be accomplished." Do I not speak the truth?

How can the Rider on the White Horse stand against us on that day if we are merely carrying out divine justice? We do not destroy only the just, the innocent, the pure; we also take those who deserve their extinction. Is this not what "god" takes as "god's" own at the end? So, I ask, how can those who act in our name ever be judged? Why, according to the book of Job, you could even see us as instruments of justice. I have a role to play. I am important to the whole process.

From where I sit, there is not enough killing, and in this we must be in agreement with our enemy, for their texts say that on that day the streets will flow with the blood of those who opposed the saints. Have we ever launched a war, an insurrection, or a revolution that was not for the good of the people? We seek to liberate the masses, so why is our goal so different? Is it not the case that at the end of time our enemy establishes the divine realm with coercion, imposed on an unwilling populace? Where is the free will in that?

POSTED BY BLZBB AT 12:01 AM, 03/03
TAGS: APOCALYPSE | NOAH | LAST DAYS

## Utopia May Be No Place to Them, but to Us It Feels Like Home

We like perfection, basically. We can use the concept of the perfect and just society to acquire yet more real estate in their minds and hearts. All we have to do is implant in their minds the desire for the absolute reign of justice, faith in heaven and earth, and love—burning love for all of humankind—in the abstract, of course. Once this is done, their revolutions cease to be the historical eruptions of the masses who want more and desire what the other has; rather, they become the establishment of the New Jerusalem, in whose blood the stains of the criminal are washed. It can be a fine line that separates love and cruelty, but there you have it.

POSTED BY BLZBB AT 4:39 AM, 04/03
TAGS: THOMAS MORE, *UTOPIA*

## On Discipline

I find it interesting that the word *discipline* was invoked by so many of you concerning the posts on torture. I think too many of you are enamored of that word. It cuts both ways, and that represents a mixed bag for us. You saw clearly what I was getting at with torture. It is a power that disciplines the body and helps the state convince its citizens that torture is a "regrettable but necessary" action to make bodies behave the way power desires.

It inscribes obedience not only on the body being tortured but also on those who fear such an event occurring in their lives. As such, it becomes a discipline that the state finds helpful to instill in the social body on occasion, especially when the order of the state is in question. In this way, the state performs in a way that pleases us.

And, as we have mentioned previously, the state is most concerned with bodies, and, by extension, consciences. But the truth is that once the state controls your body, they usually control your conscience. How often they mirror us in this regard is something we can only marvel at and rejoice in. Control of the body has always been one of our beachheads in the ongoing acquisition of space among the humans.

Remember when we offered this power to the BODY in the desert? He knew we were right; he did not refute the temptation. Control a human's body and you control their freedom. Control their appetites and you control their conscience. Oh, sure, they will be free, but only after they have been fed. Very few of them have been able to exercise their freedom in the face of want and deprivation; very few have been able to feed on something other than food for the body. We ourselves can only feed on certain lives; others are unpalatable to us.

And this brings me to the topic of why discipline is a sword that cuts both ways. There is a discipline that brings us great misery. Remember when I said that we seek to establish the discipline of control by working from the outside in? This is why torture is so effective. Well, the discipline of the secret, the discipline that our opponent employs, is often the only thing that has been able to resist the discipline of compulsion we seek to instill. And while we seek to inscribe their bodies with impulses that tie them to us, our rival seeks to write upon their lives a different story and a different reality. And this story becomes no less public than ours.

The cultivation of "god's" discipline has always been a problem for us. We prefer the unmitigated freedom, the rebellion against constraint, and the lack of any discipline. We have engaged for millennia with various strategies to accomplish the triumph of freedom, but some manage to slip through our nets. They realize that the cultivation of spiritual strength is a freedom of its own. So they cultivate disciplines of love, truth telling, bearing wrongs patiently, forgiveness, vulnerability with strength, reconciliation with others, and, ugh, peace. These few become resistant to our strategies.

I hate this because these persons become freer than ever, freer than anything the orders of their lives can deliver. They unhook from all that which seeks to define them on an external basis. To the extent they do this well they end up connected to our enemy. These people become harder for us to manage because they become ones who are able to live through the pain and suffering of their lives and not let it shape them as we would wish. We are unable to nourish the slights and injustices they suffer in order to goad them into violence. If they stay at this long enough they actually become immune to our strategies for how to live life.

Consider Mandela. We thought twenty-six years in prison would have created someone useful to us. Nursing the injustices of imprisonment, we felt sure when he came out that he would cause such a stir in South Africa that we would see thousands die in violent spasms. We were licking our chops at that possibility, but then it didn't work out at all like we hoped. We still don't know what happened, but all our plans had to be put on hold. Seeking reconciliation rather than revenge? How could we have failed so badly? I can assure you someone paid for that one.

And it is not just him. There are others, some known among the humans and some who will never be famous to them, though they are notorious in our circles. They showed such freedom in circumstances that would have broken lesser beings. I wanted to break them, but they continued to save lives during massacres on the African plains, or in the European ghettos. Sometimes they even offered their own lives in hopes that others would survive. The rest of the world would never hear of them, but it didn't matter.

I must get back to the issue at hand. We must use everything at our disposal to keep them from cultivating this discipline in their own lives. Luckily for us this is pretty easily done, especially today. There are so many more things to occupy their attention. We have managed to take their very clever development of technology and turn this in our direction. As one of them observed, they are quite literally amusing themselves to death. Being so attentive to games, celebrities, amusements, and politics (which, let's face it, is like catnip to most of them, even though many are fairly ignorant about what is really going on), they don't see the necessity of being truly attentive to life.

POSTED BY BLZBB AT 4:20 PM, 05/03
TAGS: RAOUL WALLENBERG | NELSON MANDELA | ANC | PAUL RUSESABAGINA | ANDRÉ AND MAGDA TROCMÉ | DR. JAN KARSKI | XBOX

....................................................................................................

# Living as if "God" Does Not Exist—Priceless

Some of you seem confused by things that I have written earlier. I hate to get in the weeds on this kind of thing, but I suppose it is worth going over again. We are pleased where they have ended up.

All in all, we are as happy with the progress of the last four centuries as they are. We have kept up with their advancement, and who can deny that they have come some distance? Oh, sure, the creatures believe they are casting off the chains of superstition and moving into a new era of freedom, but they have not quite got the big picture. It is because of their own egos and ethnocentricities that we have been able to blind them to that larger reality.

Still, events have moved along well enough. Some of their thinkers have traced out the contours of what has happened to them over the years and how they have shaped their lives. They have described such movement in terms of maturation. They are maturing, just not in the way they suspect. I prefer the term *aging*—like meat or cheese, something ready for consumption.

They go merrily on their way, but few stop and really think about the journey and where it leads. What things have captured their attention and formed them to be what they are? What things have they deferred, and what things have become their obsessions? They seldom even recognize how deeply they build and construct the worlds they live within. In recent years, their consciousness has developed in such a way that they are becoming more self-aware, which is always a problem for us because we want them barely sentient.

They are analyzing what the world has become as well as their interaction with and shaping of it. As long as they realize that they are creating their reality and constructing their world, there is not much harm in that. But when the more aware of them become alert to the fact that they are also creating souls, we end up losing space.

Some of them start to ask questions that make me nervous. They begin to wonder what dark reality rests within the heart of their world that they use their technologies to slaughter millions of people. They wonder about the forces that drive them to destruction. Some of them even wake up from their trance. They become too reflective, which, I don't need to remind you, is not helpful to us at all. We desire them to stay busy, very, very busy. The more spiritually aware become cognizant that something about the way the world organizes itself needs to be resisted.

They have constructed their world in such a way that we been able to find space to live. It's a complex story, and I'll have more to say later, but let's start for now with their desire for order. We want to create them as subjects for a regime that assumes absolute and total control over their lives. Contrary to popular belief, we are not that enamored of chaos. It has its uses and we love the way it eats like an acid at their souls and their societies, but we ourselves love the presence of absolute and total order. In our realm, we will not tolerate chaos. We want the worship of our authority.

They are always looking for ways to mitigate the chaos they unleash with their political and religious conflicts. One way was fashioned at the dawn of what they termed "the Enlightenment." (I love that term; it's so ironic.) This era was helpful to our ultimate goal because it established the human creature as a rational and sociable being.

They assumed that humans would want to build a social order on the basis of laws and rules, even principles that everyone could agree upon as being "reasonable." They believed that they could establish the "natural" form of law, without any informing from our enemy. We must, they thought, arrange law and social order as if "god" does not exist. Now that caught our attention!

Although others sought to bring our enemy back into the picture through reason, I was rather fond of how they built entire social orders on the foundation of "god" not existing. I must confess, I was very attracted to this. One of my greatest hopes is that they eradicate all concerns about, or sense of obligation to, our enemy from their minds and lives. Unless, of course, they soak "god" with violence. Then I don't mind if "god" is continually on their lips. In some ways this is even better for us than neglect.

It was not that they were doing our bidding; they were only trying to figure out a way to establish some social order and harmony among all the competing and conflicting claims that were ripping at their lives. Other parts of the world did not share the same dilemma as the remnants of the Holy Roman Empire, but lucky for us, the ideas that were being developed in their "Enlightenment" would have happy results.

The fact that these nascent social orders would push our rival to the periphery was for me a happy consequence of their working matters out. The fact that we, too, were moved to the margins did not really bother us all that much. We liked it that people were not worried about demons and devils anymore, except when they went to one of their horror movies.

The disenchantment of the world, the casting out of angels and demons (I stole that one) that followed their new ways of thinking, served us only too well. We always wanted to be more invisible than it appeared we were in their crude and stupid superstitions. (I must confess, it did amuse us when Martin Luther used to get so freaked out by acorns rolling across his roof that he thought it was me. That grows old after awhile, though.) A person who sees devils all the time ceases to interest us unless they become powerful. Then we have an unwitting tool ready for our use.

We loved their quest for reason and rationality. We loved that they sought universal grounds upon which to build their cultures, because once something is seen as being universal, it can usually be made into an Absolute, and Absolutes must be protected, don't you know? When they developed international law, we marveled and were not a little jealous. We had never thought of something this clever.

Do you see the trajectory now? I was slow to grasp it at first, but as it came into clearer focus I partied like it was 1599. The creatures were in search of a "natural" order, an order that any reasonable person could appeal to in the case of conflicting opinion. Because they wanted an order that was universal, everyone must, in the end, be subject to it.

I like subjugation. It doesn't matter to me ultimately what fuels it; it only matters that they are destroyed by the creations of their own hands. Though religion has always been helpful to us in this regard, we are not above using their other creations to accomplish our ends. Since politics has become their substitute for religion, we find that we can accomplish much under its auspices.

As matters have progressed, some of them rejected religion, with all its vicissitudes and conflicts, its ineffableness, and turned toward something else altogether, something that would rule them with an iron hand (for they love to be ruled as much as we love to dominate). They realized their allegiance to divinities had led them into many conflicts, but without religion where would they go? The state. That would be their new sovereign.

Of course, Rousseau, Locke, even Hobbes struggled with how to keep the state from assuming total power, but in the end they would fail. They knew enough about power to be wary of the dangers of it in human hands, but they underestimated the ability power has to assume its own goals and agendas.

All those thinkers felt that rational social beings were meant to live together in peace and harmony, respecting the properties, bodies, and rights of others. The morality of mutual respect for another's life and goods became the foundation upon which to build a society. The beauty is that Reason became such an enshrined absolute in this process that anything that did not conform to their idea of Reason became unreasonable.

Because the narratives of Reason rested on supposedly universal foundations, it could only become, in the end, totalitarian. Anyone not conforming to the sovereignty of Reason and Rationality could be dismissed as irrational. This was not seen by them as what it truly was, a creation of their own minds; rather, it was seen to be rooted in the "Natural Order" itself. It made no matter to me; what

I was so happy about was that subjects were being created that did not cultivate the disciplines of the BODY. We watched as grace and agape disappeared as quickly as citizens of Pinochet's Chile.

This is always my desire (and I should add I hope it is yours as well): the eradication of all possible elements that would instill a different spirit in the world. We don't mind the fact that they think about "god" so much; we are fine with this remaining an abstraction. We are far more uncomfortable when the spirits that respond to the call for grace, reconciliation, and love become embodied in society and culture. These persons build forms of life over which we have no control. Now *that* is a horrific turn of events.

POSTED BY BLZBB AT 4:45 PM, 08/03
TAGS: JEAN-JACQUES ROUSSEAU, *EMILE* | MACHIAVELLI | JOHN LOCKE | HUGO GROTIUS | AUGUSTO PINOCHET | DAN BROWN | *LEVIATHAN*

..................................................................................................

# The "Problem" of Evil Really Isn't One

I see that even after all these weeks the Job story still excites you. Many of you are too enamored of the misery and pain religion creates for those creatures. You rightly figure out that their unwarranted suffering demoralizes some of them. We have to be careful about this because they always seem to bounce back. But many of you are still interested in the "problem" of evil. May I remind you, we don't find it a problem—they do. For us it's a different thing.

Take the very word they use in their struggle with the issue, *theodicy*. For them it is shorthand for why the innocent suffer, but I prefer the literal meaning, the judgment of "god" in the face of suffering and evil. I think "god" owes them some accountability. It is not hard for us to steer humans in a direction of our choosing when they cry out to the heavens. You may not have caught it previously, but let me remind you that we seek first of all to make "god" an abstraction to them, a principle. In this way, much is won, because many people cannot feel the same way about a principle or abstraction the way they do about their relationships.

So anything we can do to make "god" the ultimate symbol, rather than a source of life, helps us to sow confusion. For example, think about the ways this is done with their usual arguments. They make "god" a metaphysical principle and then define their image of this principle in such ways that "god" is removed from any place in their lives. They don't realize they are doing this, but to us it has a happy result. "God" becomes their image of perfection, and that perfection becomes something that is itself abstract and meaningless.

They take something that they are familiar with—say, power—and then because "god" is perfect they take that idea and absolutize it. Power becomes all-powerful. Slap the word *omnipotence* on this idea and, voilá, we have a winner. They define what is living, nourishing, and life-giving (something we hate and despise) as something to be seen as so cold, lifeless, and abstract that it sucks out their will to live. This cannot help but turn them in our direction.

Think about how they end up phrasing the question about evil and suffering. "god" is all-powerful, "god" is all-loving, yet there is evil and suffering in the world. How then can "god" be both these things at once? Their imaginations cannot even begin to conceive of another answer, and so through metaphysical principle we remove "god" from them.

It puzzles them, this question. How could something that loves them so profoundly allow so much innocent suffering? It perplexes their writers, their philosophers, even their theologians. It vexes their poets. But because they have so identified "god" with the principle of abstraction, the principle has become "god" to them. They cannot see that "god" is *conceived* in a certain way that is really an extension of themselves. Their conception of "god" becomes the thing itself. Thing of beauty, really. They do all the heavy lifting, and we just have to come along and reap the benefits.

How many have been led into unbelief by this conundrum? Remember Dostoevsky's protest, mouthed by Ivan in *The Brothers Karamazov*? What person of sensitive soul would not side with Ivan as he recounts the innumerable horrors visited on the most innocent of innocents, babies? Who could not be moved by that protest? Why would "god" allow children to be run through with bayonets? And who, after thinking about it, would not have come to the conclusion that such a monster could not be adored, much less worshiped? Far better for us that people would still believe in our enemy but would still hate "god" for all the unnecessary pain. They have even created a name for the haters of God—misotheists. I like the sound of it, though it makes me think of sushi and soup.

Once the question gets framed in just this way, we find fertile ground. If this is the logic, how can you not end up in unbelief? Oh, sure, they try and fight rearguard actions in this. That is part of what the authors of Job were trying to work out, but the way the question is framed means that ultimately they have to come to a decision: either "god" really doesn't love them, or else "god" is something less than they have always thought. What is fascinating to me is how many of them would rather give up the idea of love than the ideology of power they have constructed their image of "god" around.

Either way, when the force of the question sinks in on them, we find them paralyzed. They cannot conceive of "god" so all-loving that "god" would be different from their definitions. The kicker is that omnipotence is so patently ridiculous an idea that it makes no sense when you start to unpack it with the most elementary thinking. How did they come up with things like "Can 'god' create a rock so heavy that 'god' can't lift it?" Real knee slappers, almost as good as their musings on how many angels can dance on the head of a pin.

Anyway, it is easy enough to turn many of them from this image and abstraction. And, in their struggle with the metaphysical abstractions, they believe they are rejecting "god," when in truth it is a constructed image they are turning away from.

Much follows from this, of course, because some of them go all in and double down. If they are going to go down the path of rejecting "god," they figure they should go all the way. That is why you have such robust figures in history whose rebellion almost matches mine. As I said before, the ones with guts looked into the abyss of their unbelief and saw the inevitable consequences of their nihilism and they went ahead and jumped anyway.

Just one more point for today. In all these years it never occurred to most of them that the images they constructed of "god" were not remotely connected to the reality of the thing itself. If they could have just wrapped their minds around that one idea, they might have found other answers to their problem with evil and suffering, but for the most part they still have not figured this out.

It never occurred to them that the One who had the power to create interstellar space, the cosmos, who had the power to nourish its coming to be, who creates all life (and here I must confess to you that we can only create death), was simply not omnipotent. No, with our enemy, power works on a whole different level than it does in their imaginations. That is all for today. I must confess that this has started to take its toll. I never imagined writing could be so draining.

POSTED BY BLZBB AT 7:59 PM, 10/03

TAGS: THEODICY | ARISTOTLE | METAPHYSICS | OMNIPOTENCE | OMNISCIENCE | PLATO | JOHN MILTON, *PARADISE LOST*

## Theodicy, Ctd.

I am finally able to take up again the topic that I had to put down. It was easy enough to write about their mistakes, but when I contemplated what is really taking place in the world, I got queasy. The disillusionment they feel in the face of such immense suffering is where we prefer they place their attention.

We don't even mind when they use religion to try and work it all out. Religion has always had ways of combating the chaos and disorder that emerges when the ugly realities of life confront them.

As we saw with the notion of karma, in some of their communities religion's main task is to keep the darkness of nihilism at the gates. Struggling with the chaos of evil and suffering, religion domesticates what they call "god" and turns it into a metaphysical principle. As I mentioned previously, an abstraction has no real connection to the depth of pain they feel when they suffer.

This is one of the reasons why their mystics have often been able to penetrate the superficialities and grasp the deeper reality. Of course, when they do this, our job is to make them look like blithering idiots. It is even better when the mystics are a threat to the religious institutions. When things go well, we are able to neutralize with derision those who have true insight.

Sometimes they help us out by being so damn obtuse no one can understand them. Remember when that German mystic Meister Eckhart said that for "god's" sake they must let go of "god"? He said that letting go of "god" was the noblest thing they could do. He didn't mean it in the way that Nietzsche did, of course, though most people were unable to figure that out at the time. Eckhart got tagged as a heretic for trying to penetrate the veil.

But he was just trying to break out of the prisons the church had put people in. When they let go of their images of what they think "god" is, they might be able to grasp a bit more of the thing itself, though there will always be that part that is hidden. This is precisely what we must be on our guard about. Letting go of their images is only the first step to liberation, and this is a journey we invest an inordinate amount of time in preventing.

Remember when Eckhart said that they love "god" the way a farmer loves his cows—because it gives him milk and cheese? I spewed on that one, I must confess. Sometimes you shouldn't read the mystics if you're drinking coffee. You could ruin your keyboard that way. Even I could not have found a more pithy indictment of their selfishness and self-centeredness. And here Freud thought he was being original with that whole projection thing. It was as brilliant in its own way as anything we have been able come up with.

This is why it becomes easy to marginalize the mystics; they do it to themselves by their attacks on all the idols the humans create to worship. As we know, the greatest power of an idol is when people are willing to kill for it. This is why we are perfectly happy with their theologies. Where does it get them in the end?

Well, anyway, I digress. My main point is that their struggle with evil often has the most positive benefits for us. Despair, disillusionment, and depression can lead to many a happy moment in our kingdom. They do not even suspect that our enemy is at work, suffering all the hurt and pain with them. It is an image they have not truly considered, and we must keep this from them at all costs.

POSTED BY BLZBB AT 3:28 AM, 12/03
TAGS: MEISTER ECKHART, *FRAGMENTS* | MYSTICISM

## Modernity, We Love It

Earlier I was trying to show you why we love the trajectory that their lives took in the last five hundred years, or ever since that vulgar monk Martin Luther unleashed the zoo they call the Reformation. I have already told you that there were important moves made to create institutions that would assume control over their lives. What they do not suspect—indeed, what has become inconceivable to them—is that an animating force emerges from all of their creations.

We want them to disregard a word like "spirit" as a relic of the past, because then they have no idea how things take concrete form. If they knew that a spirit of something, an animating force, became embedded within their creations they might give a second thought to what they are doing, but they don't manage to think ahead, not one little step. Hell, if they knew what we know, they would carefully consider every action.

In their most recent history, they made a couple of shifts that directed their lives much to our liking. Some of these we have already covered, but there is so much that we see in them that nourishes and feeds us. Remember when we said that once they stopped ordering their lives around the concerns of how others *should* be treated to one of how people can be most effectively managed, we rejoiced? This slight movement on their part opened up so much.

Instead of thinking about the ends of what they should be doing, they started thinking more pragmatically about how to behave. They developed a type of means/ends calculus that saw "rational" behavior as a way to achieve certain goals that their "rationality" had presented to them. The goal was defined by what was rationally accepted. Being "rational" meant the best way to reach this goal.

Of course, the issue of who determined what was rational was left undecided, but anyone with any type of foresight could have envisioned what came next. It is not that hard to figure out. Not only would those who possess the social power decide what was acceptable; but also, the pragmatic result was a subtle but innate atheism. Discarding "god" from their systems would lead them to value certain traits as absolutely crucial for the development of their world.

One of these traits was the notion of technique and efficiency. By paying so much attention to making sure the trains run on time, to making sure that humans could be moved around efficiently, they were creating tools we could use later. They were meticulous in building systems of bureaucracy that made sure the purely human never touched anything.

You can guess what came next, right? If all the trains run on time, and all the ovens are working at just the right amount of efficiency, and we have figured out just the right amount of gas to use so that nothing is wasted, well, then, we have a perfectly "rational" response to the "problem" of the Jews.

You see, the most powerful in the culture, the most educated, the most "rational" and technocratic became so locked into their rationality that they were unable to even think about another way of life than the one they created for themselves. They fashioned cages of iron that would imprison them in their constructions, and we didn't have to raise a finger.

After they made these shifts, the new barbarism took its place. We watched as their ambitions—say, to be the greatest architect alive—connected with those who would grant them these wishes.

Adolf Hitler, meet Albert Speer. In our version of the world, humans participate in the most heinous of crimes against humanity without a thought as to what they are really involved in. It is just "rational" behavior, after all.

Their lives have been shaped and formed by a spirit they cannot even begin to grasp. "Rationality" has come to dominate their world in such a way that it challenges even religion for supremacy. Their rationality tells them if they can do something, they must; it never really asks them whether or not what they can do is harmful or beneficial to them.

They no longer see themselves defined by anything other than the social structures they live under. That disenchantment that they so embraced has removed them from the orbit of our enemy. Our flag has been planted. It's only a matter of time before our kingdom reigns over all life.

As they matured historically, they developed a consciousness that believed their lives should be defined by influences other than the spirit. As I pointed out earlier, the very suspicion of power that modernity created drove them into the arms of a self-authenticating power grounded in reason and rationality—the state.

Now, post-Holocaust, we are seeing the cracks in their wonderful edifice, but I believe we can ride this train for another good century or so. Their autonomy has made them far more concerned about what happens in this world than the next, and while this is precisely what our enemy wants, we want to focus their attention on entirely different things. We want them to think they are setting themselves free, but freedom from what? They never stop to ask that question. And we must make sure that they never do.

POSTED BY BLZBB AT 11:39 PM, 15/03
TAGS: SHOAH | ZYGMUNT BAUMAN | ALBERT SPEER

# Freedom Is Just Another Word for Nothing Left to Lose

One of you wrote in response to my last posting:

*I am a bit confused because it seems like reason and rationality release them from the fears we seek to instill in them. How does this work to our advantage? Does not the turn to reason that banishes us from their imaginations mean that we lose influence? Doesn't their freedom from us mean we become ineffective?*

This question shows how limited you can be in your thinking. Of course, freedom is one of our greatest lures. It becomes for some so overwhelming that they will fight and kill for it. They will create songs, poems, and art to extol its virtues and power. They will be deeply moved by freedom and inspired to great achievements.

We prefer to define the terms of that freedom and ensure that they define themselves by the terms we decide upon. In just this way, we can make freedom a type of cage that ironically imprisons them. I have said this before, but here we are again, which makes me wonder about you all sometimes. Though true freedom is not the fulfilling of their desires, no matter what they may think, we can use those desires to make freedom a fleeting and elusive thing.

Presently, they are free only to the extent that they are constrained by those things to which they give their allegiances. They are free in our realm when we set the conditions. In this way, they are free when they have enough money, free only if they are unchained from any other personal commitments, free only when "the Man" is not breathing down their necks, free to enjoy the best in material wealth. You should see how that works, I hope.

You know as well as I that these "freedoms" only pull them deeper and deeper into slavery. They become slaves to a self that is not a true self, or they become prisoners to images of the body created for them by others who define what beauty is. If all goes well, they end up slaves to the social structures they live within. These temporal structures create a world of superficiality and offer the illusion of things that are ultimate in order that they might give their constructed world unquestioned authority over their lives.

Freedom as we desire it turns them into slaves to that which we have always felt affection—their own delusions about what is real and valuable and what is not.

We certainly don't want their freedom to occur according to the terms our opponent desires. Our rival wants them to have personal freedom, but it is a freedom that is not rooted in the fleeting and impermanent aspects of their lives. Knowing those structures are merely transitory, "god" desires a freedom in human creatures that is open to the world and life as being the manifestations of divine becoming. We must prevent them from seeing that authentic freedom is rooted in the life that draws all things to itself.

True freedom rests on a more secure foundation than the one we wish to construct. We want them to believe that freedom is only found in their political or economic structures and that they must fight to secure those. We don't want them to suspect that freedom emerges on the basis of something far different from what time and history have delivered to them.

We especially don't want them to learn that freedom emerges in the person's becoming more human, and thus more divine. We don't want them to know that freedom means leaving the individual behind so that they may become more of a human being. If they do this, they will see their freedom is ultimately tied up in the freedom of others to be shaped by the one we hate. It's enough to make me want to vomit.

They must not leave the superficiality of our world and enter into something more substantial and threatening to us. Can you imagine the chaos, the lack of order that would result if they stopped defining themselves in terms of their culture and started to respond freely to the call of love and reconciliation?

This explains why our attacks and assaults on those who end up choosing our enemy's path must be so virulent. We must do everything in our power to portray them as true betrayers of their nation, state, tribe, or, even better, of humanity itself. We want those who embrace the delusions of our enemy to be seen as traitors to the human race. Fortunately, they make this easy for us most of the time.

POSTED BY BLZBB AT 3:29 AM, 18/03
TAGS: KRIS KRISTOFFERSON | JANIS JOPLIN | FREEDOM | DESMOND TUTU

. . . . . . . . . . . . . . . . . . . . . . . . . . . . . . . . . . . . . . . . . . . . . . . . . . . . . . . . . . . . . . . . . . . . . . . . . . . . . . . . . . . . . . . .

# Oh, the Irony

Just a brief follow-up to the last post, and I don't want to say much more about this because it irritates me to no end. What we desire and seek to elevate in their lives is the principle that freedom becomes the universal and all-encompassing goal of life. At the same time that they proclaim this to be the case, they bring their rulers their consciences and wills, placing them under their law because they recognize that they are too weak for freedom. In this way we can mimic everything our enemy desires for them.

Seeking freedom, they will build in the world the manifestations of our spirits. We will watch as they create a world of fear and terror, a glorious world of confinement, a world of total surveillance, bigger and better prisons, all done in the name of freedom. This is the space we seek, the space that starts in their minds and works itself out into the material world. Not trusting their freedom, they will build cultures of surveillance cameras, data mining, snooping and snitching. And this will be done in the promise that they will be free. What type of freedom truly comes at this price?

Some say the eyes are the windows of the soul, but I must say, I think politics are windows to the character of a society.

POSTED BY BLZBB AT 7:45 AM, 18/03
TAGS: PANOPTICON | JEREMY BENTHAM | MICHEL FOUCAULT

..........................................................................................

# I Pledge Allegiance to . . .

I was telling you about the way that humans built their new world, and some of you are so excited you act like it is the best bedtime story ever. I suppose it is, but we cannot say with certainty it will have a happy ending. I have been suggesting that the political orders became the prominent authority in their lives because they built these upon reason and rationality. The state becomes the only thing anyone can agree on. (Well, there is also science, but we'll take that one up later.) There will always be some disagreement about the form the state takes, but everyone agrees there must be government of some sort, though lately there have been some who doubt the need for government at all. It works best for us when they confuse the need for order with the existence of the state.

The created state of the Western world was what guaranteed them freedom from and independence of one another. The way the logic unfolded throughout the years allowed us to keep separating them from one another. But even as they were promised freedom in the state, that very state assumed control over their bodies. Why they don't see this is a mystery to us. But there it is and we see the way it has worked itself out.

The citizens of the state invest it with the power to regulate persons so they might be secure. But in order to protect them from one another, the state must assume increasing control of their lives. What starts out as something that seems so innocent will eventually end up just where we hope—in absolute control and dominance of their bodies, and if all goes well, their souls.

Now notice, colleagues, how this works for our purposes. Those who believe in our enemy had to vacate almost all public space in the world because religion was seen as a disruptive force. Since reason can decide conflicts and revelation cannot, reason wins. Given the conflicts they endured because religion became a useful tool in the wars of power, it was only inevitable that they would need something else to mediate the disputes. The church sought some space in this process, of course, but it was only allowed what the emerging state gave it. The state took the body, and the church took the soul, but in truth the state took both; it only allowed the church to believe it had the soul.

The church had only itself to blame for this because they had defined themselves in relation to the emperor's throne for hundreds of years. The church assumed the means of coercion to shape people's lives, but they neglected the means mentioned above that the enemy uses, spiritual and internal discipline. The church lost the ability to truly define people's lives because the state established itself as the bearer of values under which all must live in a "rational" society.

And what were those values? Let us review—enlightened self-interest, rational control of the world, bureaucratic efficiency, and technological expertise. Now think about this carefully for just a minute. What were our twin towers of death built on in the last century? Was it not just these habits of thought we saw come to such fruition for us in Germany? In truth, what happened there could have occurred almost anywhere else. The state became the prominent actor in guaranteeing persons their security, but at what cost? The state assumed such absolute dominance because its very citizens invested it with that power.

So, I want to make the argument that humans are so weak, so venal, so without redeeming quality whatsoever that they need force and control to keep them in line. I have always argued that this is a far better application of power than love, no matter what our rival says. Historically speaking, though, who do you think has the better of it? When faced with the choice of love, protest, and resistance or obedience and timidity, we find fear usually trumps love. Well, am I right?

Do you think in their willful blindness they even bothered to ask what went on in the tall and sturdy pines beyond the boundaries of the village? Did they ask questions about why the train tracks seemed to run to nowhere? Did they even notice the acrid smell and smoke that wafted over their villages when the bodies were burned? Was resistance to the powers that brought these things into their world even a part of their identity? To be a good citizen is to be an obedient one. These are words to live by, my dark flock, words to live by. Whose spirit do you think reigned on that day?

I'll leave it for you to sort out (I know, rhetorical device, there is only one answer), but for now think of how we have been so wildly successful at reaching our goal. We have been able to elevate the contingent, the historical and transitory, and make it something for which they will give their lives. They will even turn over the power they possess to save one another from destruction. This is allowing us to build our greatest masterpiece, our great secret.

To even question the orders of state or economics puts one outside the society. Asking whether their armies, their military-industrial complexes, their secret agencies, their presidents, premiers, even their clerics, are legitimate puts one outside the village—secular excommunication.

Sure, there are many states that do not participate directly in the type of worldwide impact we wish to make, and some of those even have the best interests of their citizens at heart, but really, who cares about them? I mean everybody wants to live in New Zealand, but does anybody pay any attention to the Kiwis? Well, I suppose they do when rugby is involved, but other than that? The important thing to focus on is that very few really question whether the state itself is a legitimate order. Most people just accept it, though there will always be some who do not.

To point out, as Augustine did so long ago, that the state can be more like a large-scale crime syndicate is to commit the most grievous of sins. To suggest that people actually give their lives for power and empire when the state frames it around protection of citizens and love of country is to risk being cast into outer darkness. To us it is one and the same. We don't care how the orders justify themselves in the end. Our enemy loses more and more ground in the world, and we are able to embed ourselves that much deeper into their hearts and lives.

It works for us if Caesar shapes their values and beliefs. The virtues to which they give their lives must be worthy, but we know that they are not the virtues that our opponent hopes they embrace. We want them to become shaped by the virtues of the modern world. We desire more and better bureaucrats who build a world around technique and "rational" control. This serves us well, though they little suspect it.

In this struggle for influence, comrades, we must be constantly vigilant in implanting these ideas in them. For example, binary thinking is a great habit of thought to instill in their minds. I once saw a bumper sticker that said something along the lines of "America: Love It or Leave It." If they wanted to be more accurate they should have said "Humanity: Love It or Lose It." This is perfect for us because it sets up a dichotomy that blinds them to anything that may change them. If you are not for us you are against us. Didn't the BODY say as much? Well, it is either us or "god." One of us will prevail. As one of their singing prophets proclaimed in one of his songs, "Well, it may be the devil, or it may be the Lord, but you gotta serve somebody." True that.

POSTED BY BLZBB AT 6:29 PM, 20/03
TAGS: BOB DYLAN, *SLOW TRAIN COMING*, "YOU GOTTA SERVE SOMEBODY" | THE STATE | DACHAU | AUSCHWITZ | ALL BLACKS

..................................................................................................

## The State Has No Monopoly on Violence

As I have been arguing, the historical processes have delivered them into a world where our opponent's desires for their lives really don't factor into their decisions. We can be thankful for this in some ways, but in other ways we must remain vigilant. This is why there is presently such pushback against the world they are creating. There are those, mostly inflamed with religion, who realize that something is at stake. Often they are mistaken about what exactly it is, but they know something is awry, so they fight.

We want them fighting, of course; we just want them fighting the wrong battle. We want them to think that if they can just take over the reins of government, if they can just gain power, then they can set this thing right. Truth be told, there is an attraction in rebellion for us because of all the reasons we mentioned previously. But when their most fervently religious reach for the bomb or bullet, they heap further scorn on our rival. Why put an end to your enemy when they inflict themselves with a thousand tiny cuts?

And what better way to show how bogus religion is than when pious terrorists take up the sword of violence to bring about their pure, cleansed world? Most of the time, we want to push religion to the periphery, lest someone realize that something rests there that is so subversive to our desires it could ruin us. But if we can bring religion to the center of their attention through the use of violence, then that works just as well.

POSTED BY BLZBB AT 5:40 AM, 21/03
TAGS: CHRISTIAN IDENTITY | AL QAEDA | TALIBAN | HEZBOLLAH | GUSH EMUNIM

..........................................................................................................

# If You Can't Stand the Heat

I see that you are excited about the very crafty and subtle ways we are assuming more and more influence in the world. Some of you wonder if we would ever have another moment as sublime as the one the Austrian painter unleashed on them. Need I remind you that our greatest achievement was hidden in the horror of what he brought to the world? How they missed this only speaks to the truths I have been trying to get you to grasp.

First of all, may I take a moment of personal privilege to brag a bit? Violence, what is it good for? Absolutely everything, hah! Has there ever been anyone better at violence than us? Violence is the coin of our realm, and we trade in it everyday. It is one of the counterfeits we offer to the excitement that our enemy desires for them. We make it transcendent. It lifts people out of their everyday surroundings and offers them a world infused with meaning. It takes a thing in them that they seek to control and unleashes it.

Their propensity for violence wreaks havoc and destruction on an unimagined scale. (Well, *we* imagine it, but they don't, or else they wouldn't go down this road.) And this is only the violence they see; the other kind, which I shall write about later, is even worse.

I previously mentioned the twin towers upon which we are building our kingdom. It was obvious in their last world war what one of these towers would be, but what has remained hidden from them is what I consider our greatest accomplishment. A modern-day miracle, if I don't say so myself. I am speaking, of course, of the other event that took place during their last world war, the splitting of the atom.

In order to grasp fully the depth of this, you must go back with me to the garden, the wonderful story of their expulsion. Think about how clever the author was to put the tree of knowledge of good and evil in the midst of the story. How often they overlook that little fact. We certainly know how insightful the author was in putting me in the middle of the decisions taken.

The author was also wise in his understanding of humans. Their desire to *know*, to grasp, and then, because they know, to control, causes them to blunder wildly, wielding their knowledge like a club to beat others. You have to love that. They are so curious, and this benefits us. We like the curious as much as the enemy does, provided we are able to shape their curiosity the way we desire. Curiosity must always end in the longing to control and dominate, or at least that is our aspiration.

Anyway, the primal story tells us that they are constantly overreaching. They push the boundaries, the limitations of their lives. They are the tragic story because they always overlook what is in their best interest. They are constantly attracted to the bright and sparkly thing outside their grasp. They were gifted with the ability to move toward grace, toward love, toward perfection even.

They were not exiled from perfection; they are never banished from perfection. That annoys us, but there it is.

But, instead of moving toward the destiny our enemy created for them, they turn off that path onto those more to our liking. This grasping after the boundaries, the desire to take before its proper time what would be theirs if they only had patience, that is the thing we have been able to build our entire reign on. Oh, I know the tale of the first couple and talking snake is only one of many stories about their current predicament, but damn if it isn't a true one. This is one of the reasons that we are so entertained about their fights over whether it is a literal story. As if the truth only came in one form.

We can see from this story that their innate curiosity, their desire to know, can be turned to things that are not in their best interests. This connects to what I have been trying to explain to you earlier. Their loss of true ends in the last few centuries has blinded them to the reality they have fashioned for themselves. A spirit of curiosity moves them inexorably along the path we desire. But we had no idea they would move so quickly to the place where everything would change. When they split the atom without a thought about what hell they were unleashing upon the earth I gasped, amazed at how much real estate we were about to acquire.

But there they were, having eaten of the tree of knowledge of good and evil, they grabbed hold of the tree of life (and, consequently, death). They grasped that dark energy, and from that day we have marveled. Everything was in the balance, everything. I waited with bated breath. Would they come to their senses, realize what was to come, and step back from the precipice?

Actually, it didn't take much encouragement because the whole quest was tainted from the beginning, but how sweet to us, how hell rejoiced and celebrated on that day. We danced and sang out praises to them, we celebrated and exulted in their knowledge—and their foolish stupidity. At last, sweet Lucifer, at last, our deepest wish and fondest hope had come true, for on that great and glorious day, they had released upon themselves, by their own hand, the power to accomplish what hell could not, their own destruction. A miracle of modernity if ever there was one.

And, here's the thing, they rejoiced as well! Celebrations, followed by congratulations and awards and popping champagne corks, were the order of the day. And the beautiful thing from our point of view was the first thing they did with this knowledge. They. Made. A. Bomb. Does it now come into focus, minions? They build a world on practical atheism and we reap the rewards. They didn't really think the thing through, did they? They didn't struggle with the implications, or at least not that we could tell. No, they only asked the question where and when, not should or should not. Given their track record, it was only a matter of time before they fell into our hands.

What a glorious day in hell that was when they unleashed that horror on the world. I can still remember the absolute and utter terror and pain they suffered. There is nothing like the smell of burning flesh and boiling blood in the morning. It smells like victory. Or at least that was the word they used after the fireball. It was exquisite, the vaporizing and extinction of countless numbers was just as delicious for us as it secretly was for some of them. The terror and fear in their eyes, the "What the hell?" on their lips as they unknowingly worshiped our power that day. Thousands of innocents gone in a moment, and a door opened to us that had previously been closed.

We stood tall on that day. It made my accusation of Job seem trivial by comparison. On that day, we stood up and accused "god," "How could you allow them THIS much freedom?" We deserved an answer, didn't we? We waited for an answer, but none was forthcoming. We wait still.

Yes, in that moment I had my first real glimpse that our kingdom of desolation, our very own apocalypse, was at hand. What I have sought since the beginning of their time was within our reach because they could not stop their reaching. This is why they are so dear to us, why we would take them under our wings. We understand them, we recognize them, we see ourselves in them. Can our enemy say that? Maybe with a few, but the numbers are on our side.

Look at where the bomb led them. Nothing is the same as it was before that day, and now they are more susceptible to us than ever. Have they not lived in fear ever since? Have they not arranged the entirety of their lives around either obtaining this dark energy or preventing others from having it? Does it not constitute the great absolute engine that drives them toward the abyss? This has been our Sistine Chapel and Mozart *Requiem* wrapped into one extraordinary package. In this moment, they created *our* deepest desire, and hell rejoiced.

The fact that this event has become absolutely internalized by them and now drives their world is truly our greatest triumph. We were hopeful for quite some time that they would have finished off the job they started, and we have not succeeded at that fine and great goal yet, but we are much closer. We thought in the days after they devised the doctrine of **M**utually **A**ssured **D**estruction, they might take a closer look at the acronym and realize the irony, but they didn't. That one gave us quite a few laughs, I am telling you.

In more recent times, we have been gearing up for another pass at things. You know what they say, when one door closes another one opens, right? We just have to stay optimistic and hope that they keep pushing open the doors closed to them. Even now we are seeing new openings, new possibilities emerging everyday. If they are anything, they are ingenious, you have to give them that.

It seems that the desperate and bitter (as well as the deranged and delusional) seem determined to one day unleash that dark power again. But, truth be told, rational and enlightened, or desperate and ignorant, we don't really care who does what to whom; we only care that death, destruction, and suffering consume them . . .

POSTED BY BLZBB AT 2:39 AM, 23/03
TAGS: HIROSHIMA | NAGASAKI | MANHATTAN PROJECT

......................................................................................................

## Necessity May Be the Mother of Invention, but They're Still Orphans

Well, sorry I broke things off, but contemplating the recent turn of events in human life was too exciting, and I lost my composure. I can continue now that I have calmed down a bit.

In their decisions, they have embraced the true logic of hell. This is our great secret. You see, the splitting of the atom has made possible the means of their destruction, and for that we are truly grateful. What is even better is that this is not just a good; it has become a *necessity*. They believe they *must* have this power to defend their world. They possess the power to destroy themselves and all other life on that miserable ball of dirt, not because they choose to, but because they believe it is imperative for their survival. Irony may not be dead among them, but it is on suicide watch.

They have embedded within their world the logic of hell and are unable to see it. All they know is that some must have this power and others must not. This only leads them further into the morass because those that don't have the power of destruction believe they are at the mercy of those who do. The ones who have not joined the club think they must have the bomb or suffer threat and blackmail at the hands of the powerful. All we need is patience because at some point they will stumble into our happily waiting embrace, the one that suffocates them. This is not even the most sublime aspect of their blindness.

This horror they unleashed with their own hands carries the potential for destruction even worse than the Holocaust, and they do not recognize it. Indeed, they have so acclimated themselves to the poison in their system that they do not feel the deadening of the limbs, the numbing of the mind, the extinction of social imagination. Few among them really question whether dropping the atom bomb was ethical, was an act as morally horrific as the murder of millions of Jews. No one admits it was, in truth, a crime against humanity. But, then, no one sees that about war in the first place.

The ones that do see what true reality looks like we just tar with the unserious brush. They are not true "serious" people the way the "great ones" among them are. They won, and that is all that matters.

Any question about the morality of the act, any thought that maybe it was as little justified as the gas ovens, is met by blank stares and anger. How indignant they get if the question is raised. "Well, of course," the answer comes, "we didn't start it, but we sure as hell finished it, so suck on that." You can see the anger when one of them suggests that all the rationale offered doesn't measure up to the deaths of so many innocents that day. "They deserved it, they started it. If we had not done that to them, they would have done it to us." These words are sweet to our ears because it means that they have learned nothing, absolutely nothing.

They cannot live without the beast in their midst any longer, but instead of its being a matter of something that can or cannot be, now it *has* to be. The compulsion of it suits us, and the ongoing justification of it entertains us because when all is said and done and they stand in our realm their excuses and justifications will mean nothing. We don't care why they destroyed one another, only that they did and continue to do it. How many crimes have been cloaked with the phrase, "It was necessary," or the one I love even more, "We had no other choice"? There are always other choices, just not the ones they want to make.

So you can now understand the ways we make space for ourselves in the world. We watched as they put a face of evil to a particular type of atrocity, the extinction of millions, while the ultimate evil, the ability to destroy their entire world with its billions numerous times over, went by them in the name of the ultimate good. The world, rightfully horrified at the Holocaust, has constructed itself around the greater evil, potential nuclear annihilation.

They truly have been exiled from the garden because having tasted from the tree of knowledge of good and evil they are unable to discern the difference between the two, even though they know that the distinction exists. And, with this, our kingdom on earth is secure.

POSTED BY BLZBB AT 10:03 PM, 23/03
TAGS: WWII | THOMAS FRIEDMAN | IRAN

. . . . . . . . . . . . . . . . . . . . . . . . . . . . . . . . . . . . . . . . . . . . . . . . . . . . . . . . . . . . . . . . . . . . . . . . . . . . . . . . . . . . . . . . . . .

# It Is the Lack of Money That Is the Root of Evil

Though money is a taboo among them, we can talk freely, colleagues. I love the way the creatures have developed their economic orders if for no other reason than they also are built on the death of "god." By this I mean that they have constructed their lives around logics and rationalities that leave no room for consideration about whether their creations are what our enemy desires for them.

Since their economic systems function very well on their own steam, "god" becomes superfluous. They have come to see that markets function better if they are devoid of anything like religion. In fact, that is the genius of the orders they have created. They are able to have what they think are peaceful and ordered economic exchanges in the absence of any religious consensus. Religion just gets in the way, because the fanatics are always prattling on about justice, the poor, and usury. Those who side with our enemy want to bring justice into something that functions just fine without it. Well, for those at the top of the food chain, it functions just fine.

We want them to construct the markets in just the way they have because we don't want them to think that they are responsible to something else other than money. Remember what I said earlier about the individual? We want the notion of the individual to become absolute to them. With their fixation on the individual, they erode any sense of community among persons.

The move to accentuate their individuality allows them to be more easily manipulated. Their fear of loss makes them fearful of each other. They worry that someone will get what one of them possesses, or they dread that they will not be able to support themselves. The rich fear that laws will level the playing field and erode their wealth, while the poor fear they will never have access to the field at all.

As they all seek only their own well-being, they lose sight of the larger community, and thus all possibility of emotional bonding disappears. We want them to build economic structures that erode a sense of community. They must never think of sharing so that a larger community may benefit. The best thing for us is that they regard any claim on their lives by a larger community as evil. It is even better when our enemy becomes invisible to them as they build their economic orders.

We enjoy it when they coldly regard one other as threats to what they have. We love it when they are fixed on their own interests and desires. Because they do want community, they create false senses of it with appeals to ethnicity or nationality. In doing all this, they don't see what our opponent sees. Ultimately, they are all, every last one of them, in this thing together. But this is something we do not want them to take seriously. Better for us that they stay at one another's throats. It's worked so well in the past.

POSTED BY BLZBB AT 9:21 AM, 24/03
TAGS: THE REVEREND IKE | FREE MARKET

## The Good Life

Many of them pursue what they laughingly call "the good life." The truly "good life" is not found where they think it is, though, and the fact that they could even have one makes me vomit a little in my mouth. I do want them to think a "good life" can only be defined in economic terms and not on the basis of the community of persons that surrounds them.

In fact, I want them to define themselves on the basis of the things that they consume. This reflects our world to a great extent. We exist to consume things; it is a great pleasure for us. But we want their very identities constructed by the things they possess. Their things should shape them, not the character of their lives. We want them to shape their opinions of one another over what they wear, what they eat, what type of car they drive, or where they live. In this way, they become something completely different from what they were created for.

They are no longer formed by their interactions with larger communities but become shut up in the cocoon of stuff. We like stuff. This stuff separates them from all that is truly important because they become impersonal to one another. As I have said repeatedly, we want them to worship the individual, because the individual is an abstraction. It is the person standing in front of them that we want to make invisible. We don't want persons of unique worth; we want individuals who get to have freedom—the freedom to choose those things they desire to consume and that will, in turn, consume them.

How many marketing campaigns have been run on the siren's call to freedom? How many ads have been created promising something that ultimately is an illusion of that freedom they so desperately want? But what freedom is offered to them, really? It is the freedom of dozens of toothpastes, hair colors, or body deodorants—in other words, no freedom at all.

The true freedom of defining yourself on a basis different from the ones that the state and market allow for—well now, that just doesn't make any sense, does it? And if there is one thing we want for them, it is to live their lives on the basis of "common sense," because the more they do so the further away they are from the truth. Now that's the good life, at least for us.

POSTED BY BLZBB AT 11:02 PM, 25/03
TAGS: ADVERTISING | DOLCE AND GABBANA | VERSACE | DIOR | ARMANI

...................................................................................................

# Talk to the (Invisible) Hand

What rests hidden away from them are the countless millions in the world who exist on the margins of their "supernaturally" powered markets. (I especially like that whole "invisible hand" concept.

People who wouldn't have a clue about "god" create a force every bit as much an article of faith as religion and invest it with so much that pleases us.) We see these others in all their invisibility—those who stand on the streets of the cities selling vegetables in hopes that they won't have to sell themselves, or the factory worker making a shoe the cost of which is a month's salary, or the ones who do end up selling themselves when all they wanted was to become a teacher. These are ghosts and whispers locked inside the machine that grinds their lives into powder.

This is the shadow side of their world, of their good life. Although they don't realize it, these are the signs of violence built into their economic orders. They can't really see this, though, just like they can't see those deep in Guguletu, South Africa, who live amid squalor in tarpaper and tin shacks. The masters of commerce don't realize the hidden costs when peasants are uprooted from their homes and moved from the mountains to the jungle floors of Bolivia in order to populate a road that is being built so Brazil doesn't encroach on their territory. Or, maybe they do, which is even more delightful to us isn't it?

But, of course, when the institutions created by the masters that perpetuate these conditions make their reports to the world, it ends up being "South Africa is financially sound and the prospects are good for investment" or "Our road to Brazil's borders is going very well and should be completed within the decade." Do you see? A world is created where reality doesn't break through to disturb the inhabitants of that world. This is the world that is created where persons disappear, a world where "god" finds no purchase. In short, a world much to our liking.

It is a little bit like what their academics do when they look at history. In their desire to be objective (because let's face it, that is what they work so hard to be), the actual persons they are exploring disappear. Real persons vanish underneath the latest methodologies and purported objectivity of the scholar. Real persons often don't fit with theories about the economies and algorithms that presently drive thinking about how people should live.

From our perspective, the "invisible hand" is more likely than not clutched around someone else's throat while the apologists of the economic ideology in place have meetings, make decisions, and silently watch as lives slip off the screen of their concerns. Another win for us.

POSTED BY BLZBB AT 5:15 AM, 26/03

TAGS: ADAM SMITH, *THE WEALTH OF NATIONS* | NIKE | MARGARET ATWOOD, *THE HANDMAID'S TALE*

........................................................................................

# Efficiencies

We want them to be efficient. We want them to think of their lives in terms of efficiency. We saw them take a big step in this direction when the idea of material and efficient causes became more important to them than final ones. Once they gave up on the notion that the order of their lives should have ends grounded in something other than matter, we saw a great advance. The question of efficiency should dominate all their thinking and actions.

"Should we have a minimum wage?" "I don't know, is it efficient to the workings of the market?" "Should we have a market for people to sell their organs?" "I don't know, is it efficient to the workings of the market?" "Should we have a company where we can sell babies?" "I don't know, what would be the efficiency of such a thing?" See? Once the argument centers itself on efficiency and economic exchange becomes the primary consideration, well, everything is up for grabs, isn't it? Even human beings themselves look different under this light.

Eventually, what we want is for them to become commodities to one another. If we can get them to move onto this ground, we have great cause for hope that events will take their due course. It's the real-life consequences of this that we don't want them to think about. "Yes, it does mean that your child dies of this liver cancer, but our tables show it is just not an efficient use of our company's funds to pay for that transplant. It's just not efficient and rational. We are sure you don't want to be irrational about this, right?"

Any other consideration becomes messy. "Charity? Justice? These are far too fuzzy for us to take those into our calculations. You can't just look at the benefits, after all, there are costs to consider here. We don't want to be selfish, do we? I don't think anyone wants that."

Fix it into their minds that it is some type of natural and immutable law that income is the product of invisible forces which dictate that whatever a person gains is directly related to the amount of wealth they create, and let that be a standard against which all things are measured. It must be perceived as a "natural" consequence of life that efficiencies are the standard on which to judge the values of things. "This is not the way we *choose* society to function; rather, it is the way that markets developed according to inviolate rules of nature. We really had little to do it with ourselves." Exquisite!

Remember that, no matter the formula they find for it, no matter how they situate it, matters interpreted through the lenses of efficiency cloak this one little fact: modern economics is built on desire, the desire for more than one needs, the desire that is never able to be satiated because behind it stands the bottomless well of their wants. And, most assuredly, it is not built on the desires of our opponent for them.

POSTED BY BLZBB AT 9:54 PM, 27/03
TAGS: UNITED HEALTHCARE

# Almost Like Church but Better

I want to say we appreciate that there are institutions that are inclusive, unlike their religions. It is the market that offers inclusion, it is the market that transcends national boundaries, and it is the market, not their religions, that offers true ecumenicity. Religion keeps them at a distance, guarding their particular truths, but the market will establish the true universal reign. Eventually, we will sweep all of them into our web, even as we keep them in perpetual competition with one another.

We are all for inclusion; in fact, our desire for inclusion is no less than our enemy's. We do have some ideas how that inclusion is supposed to go—an inclusion of the rich against the poor, of kind against the other, of the powerful against the powerless. You can even flip those around; it makes no difference to us. We think this kind of inclusion can really lead to something beneficial for them, because, let's face it, they need the strong at the helm to bring the weak into line.

Of course, they are going to have to crush a few of the resistant tribes, nations, states, and other communities until they can bring them all under the embracing umbrella of peace and prosperity. But when this happens, when they finally gather together under the sheltering wings of their great structures of politics and economics, the communion they will celebrate will be McDonalds and Coke. It's not exactly bread and wine, but it's probably good enough for the likes of them.

POSTED BY BLZBB AT 2:02 AM, 29/03
TAGS: EUCHARIST | COUNTERFEIT | BIG MAC

## Global Grifters

What we enjoy is that the marks don't even begin to suspect that the whole order can be seen as one big con. As I mentioned in an earlier entry, it is helpful sometimes to think of nation-states as large-scale crime syndicates. Globalization creates its own grifters who love to sucker the rubes out of their money. The con favors a few at the expense of the many.

If those at the steering wheel see themselves as deserving of their great fortune, this really does us no harm. We want them to feel entitled. We don't want them to feel any conscience about their decisions. We would become anxious if we knew they were thinking about obligations to a community larger than their family.

The London stock trader going to work in the morning is not thinking she is going to make someone's life miserable today. No, she is thinking that she is going to help someone send their child to college or buy a new car, but what she doesn't see are the hidden costs paid in pain and suffering. I mean, things have gotten so out of hand that the pope has recently addressed this, but it is a measure of our great success that no one really listens to him. At least they don't in the councils of money and power.

The systems they put into place hundreds of years ago have become self-perpetuating, and they have acquired such internal force that no one grasps the impact of what is taking place.

The names they call their economic orders make no difference; we are mostly interested in the effects they have in the material world, the world where we hope to take more space. Remember, for us this is the most important thing, because the more we make all that is penultimate the ultimate, the blinder they become. The less they can see the global effects of their systems, the more space we are able to take.

In the present world, those who have income define what the world will be, those without income cannot really drive any demand beyond survival, so they don't really count in the calculations that are made about how the world is structured. The truth is, most of the poor are invisible, and life and death depend on who has the means and who doesn't. There are those few communities that try and build their society with consideration of the voiceless ones, but even those become defined by what they consume.

If some of you are skeptical, watch what happens when one of their Squawkers goes on about the corruption inherent in the system. Remember that Hebrew troublemaker Amos and his pithy critique about selling the poor for a pair of shoes and the needy for a bit of wheat? That wasn't even capitalism he was attacking, but did he ever piss them off back in the day.

No, the trick is to marginalize those voices, make them seem something akin to crazy people yelling on the street corner. When those souls who see clearly what is happening around them start pointing out the costs of the present world, push the impression that they are not realistic. Even better, use their media to slander them as socialists. Even now there are plenty of apologists for the system already yelling at the top of their lungs on the airwaves. They attack anyone who tries to bring the poor and dispossessed into the picture. We just hope that people don't see the difference between those screaming out of fear over the loss of their own prerogatives and those contesting the present orders on behalf of those who have no voice. It helps if you can build some resentment against the poor, because then no one will listen to those who seek to speak for them.

POSTED BY BLZBB AT 6:20 PM, 01/04

TAGS: *THE GRIFTERS* | *CARITAS IN VERITATE* | IMF | AMOS 8:4-6 | AYN RAND, *ATLAS SHRUGGED*

...................................................................................................................

# Fear, Inc.

We want to place fear into the heart of all that they do. We don't care what type of fear it is. Fear of difference, fear of chaos, fear of themselves, fear of each other, it doesn't matter. We even like it when some of them seek the tiny meaningless little fears of their horror movies. That just corrodes their sensitivity to violence and helps us establish it as normal.

No, we seek to embody fear in their lives in such a way that the vague can become specific. Take, for example, the fear of the other, the immigrant. Currently, this is one of our most successful works. The ones who fear so much don't realize the movement of people started in the hidden violence of their economic orders. The fearful believe that someone else is threatening to take away what is theirs. Of course, the "theirs" part is a bit ironic, seeing as how what is "theirs" was usually someone else's first until "they" came and took it.

Remember, our mission is to win space in the world, and in order to do that, we want the very concreteness of their fears made real. For example, we discovered the other day that people out in the American southwestern desert who are giving water to those making exodus from the south to El Norte are being charged with crimes against the state. I can't tell you how much this pleases us because it just allows us to give the finger to the BODY.

Who did he think he was kidding with his whole "Whoever gives a drink of water to the least of these has given it to me"? He didn't fool us because we knew the destructive potential found in those words. A drink of water, given in the right circumstances, can be one of the most subversive acts possible. It means another view of the situation exists that they don't control.

I want them to grow in a certain direction that does not cause them to question or resist the state, or the society, or the tribe. I don't want them attached to a view that contradicts the worldviews they live under. I want all life to have the value we attach to it, and that means no alternative world can exist other than what we desire. When people offer a drink of water to the thirsty that the state prohibits, this act moves persons beyond the fear we seek to embed within them. I know how subversive to our reign the drink of water can be. The only right to give water to the dying should be the one we bestow.

POSTED BY BLZBB AT 1:00 AM, 02/04

TAGS: ARIZONA | EUROPE | IMMIGRANTS | NATIVE AMERICANS | PILGRIMS

..................................................................................................

# Don't Fence Me In

What invisible fences are being built not out of malice or even fear but out of a wish to have a healthy and solitary life? The soft totalitarianism of the world exists under the demand for security. This sense of peace doesn't have to come in the form of gated communities or national fortresses; it can be housed in two-car garages where thieves cannot break in to steal, nor rust corrupt.

We like fences and walls. We love to see them constructed in the interior and exterior spaces of their lives. The exterior ones, of course, are fun to watch. The Great Wall of China, the Berlin Wall, the wall on the American and Mexican border regions, and one of my personal favorites, the wall that separates the Palestinians and Jews. People building walls to keep out their own distant relatives is just so . . . what is the word I am looking for? . . . Oh, yes, ironic.

Walls have always been built out of fear, of course, but as much as they were built to keep others out, they also have the effect of shutting others in. People are shut in on themselves when they fear that others will take what is theirs, will overturn their culture, will, in fact, kill them. This fear keeps them imprisoned within walls far stronger than those made of brick, stone, iron, or electricity.

Regardless, you can see the results of our desire to occupy space in the world etched in their landscape. But, as I've already pointed out, the space we claim on the inside of their lives will usually find its way to the surface. They will build these monuments to their terror and lay down markers of their fear, and we will marvel that they have strayed so far from home.

POSTED BY BLZBB AT 4:53 AM, 03/04
TAGS: GREAT WALL OF CHINA | BERLIN WALL

..............................................................................................

## If You Speak It, It Becomes Real

Violence is one of the ways we most effectively manage the world. As long as the majority of them remain unaware of the acidic nature of violence, they keep running like rats in a maze, or maybe better, like hamsters in a cage. We have the upper hand here, considering the infinite variety of forms that violence comes in.

Take language, for instance. Language, too, comes cloaked in necessity. You and I know how powerful a factor language is in constructing their reality, but they fail to perceive how useful language becomes when we want to take space. Language creates the distortions they come to believe are true things.

You can see this in the way they use language to create their images of other people. Think about the way some of them refer to Muslims, or others of them refer to Jews, Christians, or even atheists. Just the very tone can indicate something we appreciate. The Muslim is no longer the person who lives next door; she becomes an abstraction, painted with the same brush that colors their canvas of misperceptions, distortions, and communal assumptions. It works the same way for everybody, but the dominant in a culture decide how language works. In the right hands, language turns a person into a symbol to be feared.

Those who desire power, or those who are afraid, employ all these fears to create an image with words of something that threatens. It is the same way that language created "the Jew" or "the Negro" (of course, there are so many vicious variants of those words, but let's just leave it at that for now). The point is, what emerges is a violence that structures and shapes society, and rests in their lives like a virus only awaiting the propitious moment when it can explode into overt and objective violence, leaving bullet-ridden buildings and orphans.

POSTED BY BLZBB AT 10:39 PM, 05/04
TAGS: RACISM | STEVEN PINKER | NOAM CHOMSKY

..................................................................................................

# The Only Thing They Have to Fear Is Not Fear Itself

Since I love writing about fear, I want to expand some more on comments I made earlier. I had tried to get it through your thick skulls that fear is a very powerful weapon in our desire to create space. I used the example of the immigrant. But this can extend itself to so many other areas. The fundamentalist fears the atheist, the atheist fears the fundamentalist, the political order fears the terrorist, the terrorist fears the state, the capitalist fears losing their goods to the poor, and the poor fear the powerful. It's almost like a nursery song I once heard.

Once again, the trivial details matter little to us, only the fact that fear becomes as intense a force for arranging their lives as religious purity or the desire for more. It doesn't really matter if they sincerely believe there are good reasons for their fears. Of course there are, they created them. There is always the flood, or virus, or hurricane to worry about, but the real fear that controls them is a self-inflicted wound.

I am reminded of one of their sacred texts that proclaims something to the effect that perfect love drives away all fear. This is something else we must do our best to hide. We do not want them to discover that love could build them another world, one more resistant to our grasp. We don't mind if they love, of course, but we prefer love when it is oriented to our desires, which is to say, no love at all.

This is what so angers me about our enemy. I don't really understand how they can have faith, because what type of love does "god" offer anyway? A love that moves them beyond the territories they have etched in the ground and soul? A love that relativizes all their constructions of order? They don't know it, but this type of love will get them killed. Love didn't save the BODY when the time came, did it? How can they not see they are being manipulated?

This love demands of them different forms of life than the tolerant liberalism or orthodox conservatism they make their camps within. Is it fair to ask of them that they let go of their established lives and the orders they live under? I mean, seriously, these things have created them who they are. What right does love have to disrupt them? We want to comfort them in the midst of their lives. What has "god" done but call them out to be exiles from their own people?

In this letting go, the BODY promised them a new life, but they must die to the old one. He told them that following love would cost them their lives. Just came right out and stated it as bold as you please. If they followed love, they would suffer and die—die to ego, to attachment, to self. How effective a recruiting tool can that be? Lucky thing for us not so many have wanted to walk that road, eh?

We come along when there are those who are close to grasping the radical leave-taking this would entail and whisper those words that have been so helpful to us: "Did 'god' really say?" Since time began, this has been one of the most beautiful thoughts we have implanted in their lives. How sparse, how austere, how effective this one line has been throughout their history.

"Did 'god' really say you should turn the other cheek? Did 'god' really say you shouldn't do this thing or that thing?" Or, the one we work on the hardest, "Did 'god' really say you should love your enemy? Surely 'god' could not have meant this? Why, your enemy is the thing that is trying to take what is yours, to harm your own, how could you love that?" In our world, minions, we'll love our enemies when we see them swinging from nooses outside our bedroom window.

You see how subtle, how nuanced, how perfectly reasonable this line of argument is? Just allow this thought to grow and nourish itself for awhile in their minds. Marinade and grill, marinade and grill. "Are you and you alone right in your resisting so much of what your people have built? Aren't you really the only one protesting against the situation? Who do you think you are to say that religion is flawed? Who are you to question the political orders? Who are you to raise concerns about how wealth is used? Who are you to resist all the good and noble efforts of your colleagues and friends?"

The fear of being megalomaniacal, stubborn, not a good team player, has usually been enough to turn them away from *agape*. This is just another way in which we can use fear to notch another mark on the tree of their knowledge. Once deep into the forests of fear they have planted, it is difficult, if not impossible, to find one's way out.

POSTED BY BLZBB AT 2:40 AM, 06/04
TAGS: GENESIS | EDEN | 1 JOHN 4:18

........................................................................................

## Terrorists 'R' Us

Some of you in messages to me have been much captivated by terrorism. You seem to think that terrorism is such a reflection of our wishes that we have already succeeded irrevocably in our goal of taking space in the material world. You have to be careful here, colleagues.

Of course, we use fear of the terrorist the same way we use fear of anything else that accomplishes our purposes. It is easy enough to plant the flag of fear in their lives over the random terror and destruction brought about by seemingly senseless acts of violence. What becomes more difficult for them to discern, and something we don't want to happen, is that those who resort to acts of terror have often been pushed to it by the violence that their enemy's social orders perpetuate.

The fear of those being terrorized, of course, blinds them to the fact that conditions exist that they may not be responsible for individually but which have certain undeniable effects in the world. Because we have managed to keep evil an individual action in their minds, they seldom grasp that the very orders they created provoke the responses that will continue to perpetuate the cycles of hatred, fear, and violence that so dominate their lives.

Pushed to the brink by those forces arrayed against them, there will always be those who feel the need to resist. Often it is the marginal and the powerless who lash out against the powerful. They perceive the choice offered them is capitulate or die. It's not that they are wrong about this, but the fact that they react so spectacularly only serves to unnerve those who rule. Sometimes, and this is a mystery to us, the privileged respond to the oppression of others by renouncing their power. Frankly, their motives are hidden from us; it is difficult to figure why they would give up their privilege. It's certainly not what I would do.

Most people don't really think about the reasons for why things are the way they are, they just react when the pushback comes. The majority cannot even imagine that those who are lashing out, seeking to destroy the orders of their world, are themselves fearful of losing their very souls. Capitulation to the forces that have emerged to shape the modern world means the loss of everything they hold dear. For many of those on the outside of modernity's world, the loss of tribe or identity, even faith, are very real possibilities. The forces at work that are eroding their lives represent the erasure of their very being. We just want all parties involved, no matter which side they stand on, to feel . . . what is the current phrase they use? Oh, yes, an "existential threat."

POSTED BY BLZBB AT 10:27 PM, 07/04

TAGS: WAR ON TERROR | HINDUS AND SIKHS | TALIBAN | PAKISTAN | TAMIL TIGERS

...........................................................................

# We Are All Terrorists Now

In my last post I was trying to get you to see that terrorism is more pervasive than one might be led to believe at first glance. The dynamic is often the same, the same fears at work, but the beauty of it is that we acquire more real estate in our ongoing struggle, and they do not see it. Keep their focus on the question of why someone would act so unreasonably as to kill themselves. Have them question why someone would be so suicidal as to sacrifice their life. If we can rivet their attention to these types of questions, we are assured of endless repetition of the violence.

Do you think the citizens of Hiroshima and Nagasaki saw those who dropped those bombs as unleashing any less terror than the ones who suffered at Pearl Harbor or New York City? State terror is born of the same fears and concerns as those that drive the few who are seeking to take down the system. But the beauty, from my point of view, is that once one lives under the rule of a particular order, nothing that order does can be wrong for those who live within it.

We come back to the garden, don't we? Standing in the garden of the tree of knowledge, they think they know the difference between good and evil. Of course, what usually happens is that good and evil is constructed from the ground upon which they stand; that ground legitimates their actions. Good is my invading your country; bad is your fighting me back. Ethics, as practically worked out by them, is remarkably easy.

Keep this truth from them. All over that infernal sphere, testicles with electrodes attached await the electricity, bones are crushed, children are snuffed out, all in the name of the good. Actions taken must be seen as being for the love of country, or even faith, but never for the sheer love of power, nor the pleasure of the act of violence. No, we must keep them in the frame of mind that their violence, their heaping bowls of revenge, their bloodlust, is done for honor, for country, for "god," or most pathetically, for security.

POSTED BY BLZBB AT 3:12 AM, 08/04
TAGS: ETHICS | SUICIDE BOMBERS

# Did God Really Say?

Just one quick thought for today. When the BODY said you must love your neighbor as yourself, do you think he actually had any neighbors? Or maybe he meant for his hearers to be filled with self-loathing? This has always confused me.

POSTED BY BLZBB AT **4:23 AM, 08/04**
TAGS: **SERMON ON THE MOUNT**

# Torn Between Two Loves

I want to take a moment to respond to some of you who are debating the last few posts on terrorism. In particular, some of you are wondering about the way that threats to identity unleash terror. Consider, then, their present circumstances. We have one group of people who have been entirely shaped by the forces of modernity I mentioned earlier. Their views of rationality and technical expertise lead them to rely on themselves more than anything else.

This means that they have constructed a world that is shaped in such a way it drives all the inhabitants of that world in a certain direction. The earthly results of this shaping we know all too well, but these effects certainly transcend the boundaries they create. Humans seek expansion, they seek resources, they seek markets, they seek influence, and because they extend themselves into the world, they have impact on other communities.

Now put into the mix how different cultures respond when they come into contact with one another. Think, for example, of the pragmatic atheism of the West and the devout belief that exists in other parts of the world. Lives in these worlds have been shaped in entirely different ways. Because religion centers many people's perspectives, they don't approach life in the same way as those shaped more strenuously by the pragmatism of modernity. In fact, many of those who profess allegiance to "god" view the world of modernity suspiciously.

This is a combustible mix. One culture that believes strongly in the separation of all religion from the political order puts boots on the ground in another country that sees religion as part of the oxygen they breathe, and BOOM! While all the new conflicts are being generated from this mix, we watch with wonder at the lunacy of it all.

Those people who are religious believers sometimes see the modern world as polluting their lives. For their part, citizens of modern, secular cultures are perplexed by the anger and resistance they experience because they believe they are just bringing "the blessings of liberty" or some other benefit to the masses. It really doesn't make a difference what the intentions are, though. Chances are good that there will be an explosion because the very thing most valued by one group is seen by the other community as an insult, an affront to their very lives. How can this not combust?

Now mix in the type of ethnocentricity that keeps them from ever truly understanding one another and, with a little luck, we have exactly what we want. As we watch their history unfold, they cannot help themselves. The hidden desire for control, for power, for empire is too strong in them. If the shoe were on the other foot, if the religious ones had all the military power, well, everyone would be laying out prayer mats, wouldn't they? Is this not *the* great fear that drives them? They fear that one day the shoe may be on the other foot, and in this world no one wants to be shoeless.

As an added bonus from my perspective, many in the Muslim world don't even grasp that the West has built their society on the death of "god." The Western world is still perceived as Christian, even though we know this is certainly not the case. This really confuses people because the Western world does not really center their orders on anything remotely having to do with a "god." They have convinced themselves they are in other countries to bring the benefits of democracy, not religion. The irony is that it is their religion that is seen as a corrosive threat among some of the most devout. From a certain vantage point, the West looks like a world of apostates. I could not have set this up better myself.

POSTED BY BLZBB AT 8:29 PM, 09/04
TAGS: KUWAIT | IRAQ | IRAN | SEPARATION OF CHURCH AND STATE

........................................................................................................

# (H)ella (Dis)enchanted

When morality becomes reduced to political expediency, I rejoice. This is especially the case when the religions join together with the political. I prefer religion out on the edges except on those occasions when I want religion to take the center stage, particularly when it connects its fortunes to the desires of the powerful.

Religion can root violence, control, and deception in the center of things every bit as skillfully as political actors do, but the best part from our perspective is that religion can then be the scapegoat when needed. Religion has often been used to prevent any questions about the legitimacy of the social orders that shape people's lives, but when it is unnecessary, it is often discarded.

All appeals to religion then become delegitimized, which helps us and ensures that our opponent will never be able to establish much space for divine desires to take root and flourish. The sheer irrationality of their lives remains hidden from them. Destroying the very planet they depend upon, drowning themselves in the insanity of increasing weapons, and believing they are capable of controlling all that threatens them, well, this creates a place we love to call home.

The disenchantment of the world I have been talking about was truly an advance because who in their right mind would argue that the demonic manifests itself in their world? No one uses that language; it's just so outdated. Or, if they do, they are seen as fools and no one listens to fools. Hella cool.

POSTED BY BLZBB AT 3:29 AM, 11/04
TAGS: *SOUTH PARK* I DISENCHANTMENT I MAX WEBER I ANNE HATHAWAY I HUGH DANCY

## Question of the Day

When the Christians came to the "New World" (though it was really only new to them) to conquer the "pagans," they were horrified because they thought the people they found were cannibals. This so offended them they killed hundreds of thousands of the Incans, Mayans, and Aztecs, often burning them alive. How far of a distance do you think it is between the roasting of the live body and the eating of the dead one?

POSTED BY BLZBB AT 4:40 PM, 11/04
TAGS: CONQUISTADORS I PIZARRO I CORTÉS

# It's the Indifference We Hate

There is an aspect of some of the followers of the BODY that truly does annoy me. It is their indifference that we despise. We don't understand why they won't engage. We accuse them of being no lovers of humans, of showing no charity toward their own when they refuse to join in the orders that determine their world. They won't join a party, they won't enlist in an army, hell, some of them won't even go to a party. Take sides, dammit!

We mock them as impotent, traitorous, weak, and uncaring. "Is it not your responsibility," we whisper, "to help the have-nots? What greater service could you perform than that you become wealthy in order to help those who have nothing, or to fight the terrorists who are trying to destroy your fellow citizens? If the regime oppresses you and your friends, how can you silently stand by while your sisters and brothers suffer? Does this not make you complicit in the regime's crimes? You need to pick up a gun to protect the weak; it is the only effective way to help."

We invoke Hitler and watch them paint their enemy with that brush. We confront them with the usual "What Would You Do?" But when everybody around them is losing their minds to bloodlust or patriotism, there are those who are not moved by our call to action. It annoys us when we cannot get them to identify with the societies they are born into to the extent that those orders will control their lives. Fortunately, these are few and far between, but still, we know for certain that they are no friends of ours.

POSTED BY BLZBB AT 5:39 AM, 13/04
TAGS: DANIEL AND PHILIP BERRIGAN | MAHATMA GANDHI | DESMOND TUTU | MARTIN LUTHER KING JR.

# Spiritual but Not Religious

I am sure you have heard of the comment, "I am spiritual, but not religious." I rather like the idea, personally. Earnestly said, heartfelt in its desire not to be swept away by the bigotries and psychic violence that bedevils religion (thank you very much), this statement typifies all the ways we have in our arsenal to discredit religion and its traditions.

Though we hate the mystic for reasons I mentioned in an earlier entry, we also love her. We especially love the mystic when she stays in her private world of connection to the "spiritual" and thus maintains her spiritual purity. Spirituality is fine with us, especially when it is disconnected from deeper disciplines and community support. The types of disciplines the creatures need to cultivate discernment, to recognize the corrosive aspects of our taking space, are seldom found in the sweet comfort of their individual spirituality, because that type of spirituality is usually a reaction to traditions that have become nonsensical to them.

The reason being spiritual is so much fun is that they get to pick and choose. If something is difficult, it can be discarded. That is why so few of them are really able to endure Zen training. It is not normal to the way they know the world. Still, even this discipline, as hard as it is, more often than not has private effects.

It is those traditions that call us out that we are eager to blunt with spirituality. There is a cultivation of discipline that brings them to death, most of the time death to their own egos, but sometimes it's the death of the whole enchilada, body and ego alike. In the old days, those people who went all in became examples to the others of the reality that we despise. When one of them said the blood of the martyrs is the seed of the church, he was not far off from the truth.

But it is a sign of our advancement in the world that we do not see as many of these as we used to, and the ones who do show up, we try either to ridicule or seek to make objects of veneration. We don't want humans to think that they actually have to discipline their lives, their attitudes, their very being, to become effective in their resistance to our taking space. We want them to think it is much too hard.

Of course, we do this with the standard questions in our arsenal. "Did 'god' truly say to turn the other cheek if someone hits you? It must have been meant metaphorically." Again, who did the BODY think he was fooling? You and I know that it is absolute subversion to turn the other cheek. Why, it's even an act of aggression if you look at it in the right way, and what other perspective is there than ours? I have never stood for that type of aggression. I won't have it. If anybody's going to be dominant it's us. Strike back, I say. Hit them before they hit us. Turn the other cheek? Only after we have burned the first one off their face.

Fortunately for us, most people have a hard time walking the same road the BODY walked. Who wants to look like a sap? Who wants to be weak? It is only when they have walked in this way for some time that the truth starts to dawn on them. The way the BODY called for unleashes them from us, detaches them from the way we desire that they live in the world. Authentic spirituality for them is elusive because in the beginning it is always hard and difficult.

One more word for today: we also want them to think that this type of spirituality is best suited for the individual. We want to disconnect them from the larger community of those who would seek to follow the BODY. As Billy Corgan put it, "The killer in me is the killer in you." That's why their faith needs a larger community; it helps them stand stronger against the forces embedded within them that destroy life. Spirituality pursued without the community of faith is easily dealt with and dispensed. Discipline pursued in the community of faith makes them stronger and less susceptible to us.

POSTED BY BLZBB AT 2:20 AM, 14/04

TAGS: SMASHING PUMPKINS, *SIAMESE DREAM*, "DISARM" | ZAZEN | ANTHONY OF EGYPT | TERTULLIAN

......................................................................................

# The Amish Make Me Nervous

One of you wrote me after the last entry and asked if I could give a more direct example of what I was writing about. Dumb as dishwater and really not fit for our company, so I dealt with him in my own manner. Do any of you have a toothpick? But just in case there are more of you who need it spelled out, I am going to give you an example.

Do you remember the West Nickel Mines Amish school massacre? Most of you should remember because this was one of our most nervous moments. A man, not one of ours exactly, but willing to do our work anyway, entered into the school on an early fall morning in October. The details are unimportant except that by the time he was done five innocent girls were dead and the shooter then turned the gun on himself and pulled the trigger.

Normally we would be rejoicing at an event so absolutely horrific, so senseless. Chaos, pandemonium, insanity, all unleashed on those whom we really have no use for. We thought this was a great advance for our side. It makes it hard to believe in the goodness of our opponent when there is so much innocent suffering in the world. The fact that the victims were Amish, the most nonviolent people on the planet (well, there are the Jains, but you get the point), only made this all the more fulfilling to us.

How could anyone believe in the goodness of our enemy after that? Senseless killing unleashed on the most innocent of "god's" creatures, little girls from pacifist Christian families. October 2 was starting out as a good day for us in America, much like it does almost everywhere else in the world, where unnecessary and horrific deaths are the order of the day.

We stood back and waited for the wailing, the suffering, the pain, the anger, the bitterness, but mostly we hoped for revenge. We knew they were Amish, but we felt pretty confident when the time came they would show their true colors; humans usually do. Unfortunately, we were right, they did show their true colors, which made me feel absolutely devastated.

Here we thought we had unlimited opportunity on our hands to win space in the hearts of people closed to us, but we did not anticipate what happened next. On the very day of the shooting, with five dead and five clinging to life in hospitals, one of the elders said to the younger Amish that they must not think evil of the shooter, and another cautioned that the killer had a father, and a mother, and was now standing in front of our enemy. Oh, well, so what? A couple of old coots nobody listens to weren't really a problem for us.

But then the response snowballed, much to my dismay. Hours, mere hours after the shooting, there were Amish at the house of the shooter *comforting* the perpetrator's family. They extended such forgiveness and reconciliation to the family that they held *the shooter's family* in their arms while they grieved. Inconceivable. In the following days, they extended more compassion to the family of the shooter, Roberts, than anyone else involved. They even *set up a fund* for the family of the shooter. I mean, *holy *@#^.*

Of course, we immediately set into action to try and do damage control. We had many who would criticize the actions of forgiveness due to the fact that the shooter's family had not begged for it. We had others denigrate the act itself as the work of a "cult" who was "just weird." We tried to ensure that the power of forgiveness did not become so manifest that humans might recognize how this stops us dead in our tracks.

It was picked up by the international media, usually very good sources for us to spread the word, but this time they were spreading stories about Amish farmers holding the shooter's grandfather for an hour while he sobbed like a little baby. There was no end to the stories about the Amish attending the funeral of the shooter to offer comfort to the family. These types of actions threaten what we seek to build for our realm, which depends on the exact opposite events happening after tragedy.

We want hatred, revenge, children named Jihad, memories scorched with the images of blood and the picture of small bodies splayed on the floor. We want the images to burn themselves into the very fiber of their bodies, minds, and souls. Then, when we come calling, there is open territory to offer suggestions about how the demands of justice might be met. "Did not 'god' say an eye for an eye"?

Instead, the world saw another reality, a reality we ourselves cannot really comprehend, no matter how hard we try. They saw people who escape our grasp, who detach themselves from the accepted patterns of thinking, who are so far removed from our schemes and desires that they seem like aliens from another planet. This was not "rational" behavior in the worlds we create. And, ultimately, this is how we grabbed back our space. We marginalized them. Who could be like this? Who has this type of discipline? Would you be like this if your daughter was slaughtered? Of course not; this is only for the weak and the strange. These people are alien to your world. This behavior is not "rational."

The way of the BODY is so foreign to their experiences they do not recognize why forgiveness and compassion are so little known among them. If these things ever became habits to them, we would lose so much space in the world we would cease to exist. There would be no place for us in a world of love, compassion, forgiveness, and nonviolence. But because it is so little in evidence to them, our kingdom remains secure.

I think it is important to point out that here we have an instance of what I have been arguing for eons—"god" doesn't really care about them. Forgiveness is a suffering all of its own because the right of retribution is given away. Who has the right to take away avenging the deaths of the innocents, anyway?

It's worse than that because even forgiveness will not take them far enough. Once one has been forgiven, the desire to reconcile can still be absent. Forgiveness can still lead to a trail of enemies kept at a distance, which is fine with us. In this case, there is no real lasting damage from our perspective. The disturbing part is that the BODY takes it further and calls his followers to reconcile with the enemy as he reconciled them to "god."

But before I leave this awful episode too quickly, I do want to point out that this type of discipline can only occur within communities devoted to forming their hearts and souls around another reality than the one we seek to build. It is incredibly difficult to pull this off as a solitary individual. So you can see why I detest those communities who are serious about resisting our way in the world, but even more so when these communities are found in their religions. Anything we can do to discredit this type of thing will only benefit us in the long run.

POSTED BY BLZBB AT 1:45 AM, 15/04

TAGS: WEST NICKEL MINES SCHOOL | FORGIVENESS | RECONCILIATION | LANCASTER COUNTY

## What's Love Got to Do with It?

As I have been persistent in arguing, we want them to think in certain patterns. We don't want them reflecting on their lives to the extent they grasp that there are actually other ways to live and that other structures can be created for their lives that would yield different worlds.

If we can have their laws take prominence over their relationships, so much the better, especially if there is confusion between law and morality. Once they deal with one another on the basis of law, the whole notion of relationship escapes any consideration dangerous to our cause.

We want their world fixed and set in stone. We want them to draw the boundaries so tight they become impenetrable to one another. We don't want rules, identities, moralities that float depending upon the relationships and complexities of their lives. Make law the overwhelming reality of their lives, and let love become soft and sentimental. That way it becomes inconceivable to them that love can form their social imagination.

The idea that the moralities they themselves absolutize can be reconfigured in order to allow new spaces to open where love might grow should never even enter their thinking. All relationships must be built on rule and law, but never love.

I also want to emphasize that we are pleased when tribal affiliation becomes their dominant form of morality. Love for one's own is always a good for us, especially when it means the death of the other who is not a part of the tribe, community, or family. What we hate is when they enlarge their circle of who is part of the family. Compassion for others who are not a part of the group should be discouraged. It's too much like what the BODY wanted for them to live into.

POSTED BY BLZBB AT 4:52 AM, 16/04

TAGS: TINA TURNER | INSPECTOR JAVERT | *LES MISÉRABLES*

..................................................................................................

## Calling Down the Fire

Another thing we hate and despise about the BODY is that he embraced others so freely, so unconditionally. Even in his last moments of suffering and torment, he cried for forgiveness for those who were crucifying him. This is so foreign to our world that I suspect it must have been a ruse to confuse us. We would call down the curses of justice upon their heads. We would call down the wrath to slay them all.

It was incomprehensible to me how he was able to take whole worlds into himself, even the worlds of those who desired his death. What an insufferable wimp! It's not like he didn't tell the truth about some of those in his community. He called out the ones who resisted him in order to protect their own power. He even said they were snakes and vipers. We did find that highly amusing. He certainly seemed to know who he was dealing with, but still he never closed off the path of possibility for anyone. Victim, perpetrator, or bystander, they could all be brought into relationship if they would give up their claim to ego, power, or wealth. How can someone take that much of the world into themselves and not perish? Funny thing, he was always impervious to the tried-and-true "Did 'god' say?" strategy. Always had an answer for that one, even in the desert.

Calling down the fire of love upon them, he subverted everything they (and we) strive to build. When they lovingly construct the habitations of justice and law, unbending and unyielding order, he torches their house with love and mercy. When they painstakingly build the memorials that house the memories of centuries of war, conflict, atrocity, he brings them the hope of reconciliation. When they diligently work to erect a future of hate by building skyscrapers of revenge, he brings the flames of forgiveness to leave their work in ashes.

I ask, by what right? What right does he have to tell the victims to give up their gaping wounds and suffering? Sometimes hanging onto the pain is the only way to stay alive. What right does he possess to tell the mother who suffers the loss of her husband and all the rest of her children she cannot name the child in her womb "Revenge"? If he is truly compassionate, how can he tell her not to plot to destroy her guilty, guilty neighbor for unleashing hell upon her? What authority does he possess to confront with forgiveness and reconciliation those whom we would shelter under our wings of revenge and justice?

Does he have any idea how much suffering there is in the world? We certainly do, in minute detail. Does he have any idea how much pain they experience at the hands of one another? At least we offer them hope. We give them hope that one day justice and law will be dominant, and when that time comes their enemies will pay for what they have done.

We offer them the solace that the death of their loved ones will be avenged and the cries of the blood on the ground will be answered with the quiet swoosh of the noose, or the steady hum of electricity. At least we care about them. We don't ask of them the impossible.

But he comes along, a terrorist to all they have built. He wants to shelter them from the storms of hate and would set the torch to our world. I hate that this fire destroys the world we seek to create. We want fire, of course, but ours burns brighter because it is more public. Our fire burns crosses and houses and skyscrapers. Our fire destroys the evildoers. We raise our voices in defense of humanity, condemning that world of sentimentality to which he calls them.

Did he even care about all the pain and agony of those he purportedly came to save? Did he hear the cries of the dispossessed, the agonized moans of the tortured? At least we were going to do something to rectify matters. At least we exist to give them something other than the vague and empty promises of love. The very love that got him killed he now dares invoke in order to burn down our house?

Why would we not want to launch our hostile takeover of all that he desires? Why would we not want to colonize his realm and bring people back from madness to sanity? We have a moral obligation not to allow people to become better victims. We should not allow them to commit the type of suicide he did.

I put it to you—who loves them more? He who comes into the world with empty hands, proclaiming that those who love are born of "god"? Or is it we who come into the world with order, law, politics, and economies to feed them? What has he given them that would allow them to exist in a world of violence and might? He won't fight for them because his reign is not built on coercion, but we will. We will fight on their behalf and ask of them a small price: their souls.

Listen to me, colleagues—what we offer them in return for worshiping at our temple is home, a place of belonging, identity, a country or kingdom worth fighting for. He wants them to be willing to die for others if it becomes necessary to resist, but we want them to understand that sometimes there are things important enough worth killing for. In the end, they will turn to us; they always do, because, evidently, everybody loves a holy war.

POSTED BY BLZBB AT 3:12 AM, 18/04

TAGS: DOSTOEVSKY, *THE GRAND INQUISITOR* | MARK HEARD, "EVERYBODY LOVES A HOLY WAR"

# You Have to Crush Chickpeas to Get Hummus

Some of you couldn't help but notice that I seemed a bit more irritated than usual in my last entry. I am sure you can understand my anger here, and if you don't, then let me just say that you are not fit to live among us.

We have been discussing for quite some time the world we live in and the reasons why we can find such a home there. Of course, our primary desire is that this world is a space we can inhabit freely, with room to roam, air to breathe (all the better if there are a few mushroom clouds on the horizon), and food to feed us.

But we are also aware that we have responsibility for them in our world as well. Every prey deserves the respect of being honored, and they are no different. So we lovingly embrace them in their endeavors, sort of like a python. We don't want them to be taken advantage of by the empty promises of love.

What the BODY desires for them is beyond their ability. How can you look at history and not see this? How can people hold justice in one hand and mercy in another without there being disaster in the end? How can they live with the realization that everybody wants to see justice done to someone else? There are endless demands for justice. Once they gave up any notion that justice might be a thing rooted in a realm beyond their everyday experience, who was it that took them in? We did.

We put justice into the hands of those who would take power because they had the means to enforce it. Sure, they may have had other agendas, but this only meant they were realistic about power. You have to crush a few chickpeas to get hummus, right?

Our opponent claimed to speak for the powerless, but when he had the chance, what did he do about it? Nothing. No revolt against the government, and no rebellion against tyranny. Nothing. The BODY proved unworthy of our world, even though we gave him ample opportunity to see the error of his ways.

All through the stories of those depressing Hebrew prophets and the followers of the BODY, those who took that power we offered were continually called into question. What, are the powerless less sinful because they were too weak to serve power? Why, then, such concern for them? Why care so much for those who are enfeebled? We care for the strong, and if we don't, who will? We help those who help themselves, but "god" helps the helpless and leaves the rest to fend for themselves. Is this fair? What kind of world emerges from such a thing? No good can come of that, I assure you.

POSTED BY BLZBB AT 11:04 PM, 19/04
TAGS: EGGS/OMELET | TAHINI | PITA

..................................................................................................

# Lord of Bullshit

I have often been called the father of lies. I even heard one of you say behind my back the other day that since Beelzebub is the lord of the flies I am the Lord of Bullshit. Made me laugh, but he was tasty, I must say, so some good came out of it. But hear my side of the thing—"god" is the true father of lies if ever there was one. It is because "god" is so freaking inconsistent.

Did not "god" establish the law of no murder? Did not "god" set up the *lex talionis*? And yet what do we see in all those stories that are spread through those Jewish and Christian texts? "god" is constantly reneging on the promises of justice, and the very standard "god" supposedly creates is being overturned. How can you trust such a thing? At least we are consistent.

Think about it from our perspective for a minute. Cain kills his brother, so we figure Cain is going to get his, right? I mean, this would be the logical conclusion, even if the thing hadn't been set in stone yet. Did our rival just decide that, "Hey, you know what? I better set down some rules and commandments before they go a little crazy, and, come to think of it, they better be commandments and not suggestions." So, even though those hadn't been made public, Cain gets a pass? Cain walks? He even gets to be an urban planner with a condo and bagels on the corner. Or, at least I think they had those in Enoch. Really, what is one to think of such a thing?

Or take that little weasel David. Typical politician, you say? Well, sure, *we* thought he was a despicable little climber (the dead bodies he must have stepped over, huh?), but our opponent's opinion? Man after "god's" own heart is what we heard. Really?

Just so we get this right, someone who loves "god" sleeps with another man's wife, gets her preggers, and then, in order to cover it up, has the husband of his lover killed? Oh, sure, he didn't put in the knife, but he may as well have with his orders to Uriah's general. Someone who was so loyal to David gets murdered in the name of political expediency.

We are amazed that he has become such a template for politicians for time immemorial, but here's the main point I'm trying to make. The law says Cain deserved death, but what happens? Cain doesn't even say he's sorry and he walks. It's confusing. Where is justice or the law when it's someone "god" likes? Seems like justice is pretty shallow after all, which is why it seems to work the same way among them. The powerful walk all the time, while those who are powerless have to pay the full price for their crimes (and sometimes they don't even commit the crime). In the larger picture, we don't mind, because undeserved suffering is like an aperitif to us, but still it seems unfair somehow.

Their stories are littered with the pathetic sight of the human wreckage strewn across the landscape, but then "god" comes along and fixes them up, blesses them, and sends them on their way? Saul stands around having lox and bagels while they stone Stephen, and he isn't punished? So here's my question—why the hell do all those murdering, lying, adulterous bastards not get their just deserts? Even more, why aren't *we* forgiven? It's the injustice of the thing that just unhinges me sometimes.

POSTED BY BLZBB AT 6:02 AM, 20/04

TAGS: POLITICAL SCANDALS | MONARCHY | CAIN AND ABEL | DAVID AND BATHSHEBA | PAUL AND SAUL

........................................................................................................................

# Grace?

I have always thought this whole notion of "grace" is too clever by half. I mean, if you really look at it from our eyes, we know the truth of what is going on. In the story they tell one another about the BODY, humans are born into sin because of some primal transgression that was so great, an offense so grievous, that humans themselves are unable to repay their massive debt.

The only remedy left to them after the horror of what they have done is given to them in the great sacrifice. But how can they fail to see how despicable this is? If someone forgives you for something, you are forever in his or her debt. There is no way around it; you cannot escape the fact that you are indebted. That's the way it is with us; why should it be different with our enemy?

This works itself out in a million different relationships every day. Sacrifice is an exchange that takes place all the time. Bosses do something for their workers in order to keep them from asking for higher wages, husbands bring their wives flowers because they want sex, wives give the sex because they want jewelry. What, you think this is too cynical? I think these are the exchanges that make the world go 'round, so go ahead, prove me wrong.

Once a gift is given, they have their hooks in you, even more when it is an act of mercy. How can someone adequately respond to this? This whole business of free will is such a lie, because how could it be free if it is so carefully coerced? We understand coercion, of course—it's stock in trade for us—but what right does our enemy have to use it?

One can almost hear "god" saying, "I gave my life for you; what have you done for me lately?" I mean, who can resist that? Remember that movie with Mel Gibson? The one that was like Braveheart meets the BODY? How could you watch that and not feel the obligation? The BODY takes a bloody beating *for you*. In the face of that type of manipulation, it's astonishing some of them have had the guts to say, "No thanks."

Of course, it's also amazing that in the story they tell, those who really exercised their free will and resisted divine extortion, those who held fast to their own integrity and rejected our enemy end up spending an eternal life in a place of everlasting heat and horror, which, I suppose, if you think about it is like living in a condo in West Palm Beach. So, they have that going for them, at least.

And what of justice? They arrange their lives around their ideas of justice, but the whole idea of mercy just mucks this up, doesn't it? If someone screws with me, they should pay. I really don't want them forgiven. That's just how I roll. Who is "god" to forgive someone who wrongs me, anyway? It's sheer arrogance, it is, and

I can't understand how the idea of grace carries so much weight with them.

POSTED BY BLZBB AT 4:45 PM, 22/04

TAGS: *THE PASSION OF THE CHRIST* | MEL GIBSON | SUBSTITUTIONARY ATONEMENT | "DIAMONDS ARE A GIRL'S BEST FRIEND"

...................................................................................................

## Justice?

The thing that so mystifies me is why our enemy sees things so differently from us. We see free and rational social agents making decisions, and we judge accordingly; "god" sees the orphan abandoned at the doorstep in need of mercy and a meal. We see the justice in the once and for all, no exceptions, no allowances, three strikes and you're out. Our enemy sees a broken relationship and fluidly works to restore it on the basis of a desire we cannot even begin to comprehend.

We do not even have the suction cups to grasp the phenomenon of grace (ugh, that word makes me feel so dirty), we just don't. We don't understand the inconsistencies because in our world we strive for consistency, rigorous consistency. We don't understand partiality, either. Shouldn't "god" judge everyone impartially, the way we do? Does this mean that a world of perfect justice is a world built on love? How can this be? It's just too damn squishy a thing to rely upon.

If this is the way things are, we must gird our loins (I really miss those old-fashioned terms sometimes) and fight the good fight in the name of pure justice, universal justice, legal justice, and proclaim that because of "god's" preference for some over others, "god's" justice cannot be trusted. If "god" prefers the poor, the powerless, the dispossessed, then "god" is truly unjust.

Some of the sacred texts say that the BODY came to save all, but you can't build a world on grace and love and have things run as smoothly as they do in our world. Mercy messes up all the calculations that people make in their dealings with one another. At least in our world the trains run on time, even if they do stop at Auschwitz.

I strive to create a world of certainties, of the black and white, of the absolutes that remain absolutes and aren't changed by the whims of grace. I don't do this out of malice, I remind you, I just realize that it is more comfortable for them to live in my world. The world of grace comes along and undermines the world we seek to create. At least we're not schizophrenic, establishing divine law only to overturn it when circumstances or preferences warrant.

POSTED BY BLZBB AT **9:50 PM, 23/04**
TAGS: **LAW/GRACE | MARTIN LUTHER | JOHN RAWLS | RICHARD RORTY**

........................................................................................................

## Opposites Attract? Hardly

I am sure you have all heard the saying, "Opposites attract"? It's a romantic notion they use to talk about negotiating difference. Variety is the "spice of life" unless it's something they don't like. It's a notion we can use to disguise what is really going on because we want opposites to be at one another's throat. To a certain extent, the oppositional is useful.

It is the case, of course, that oppositions exist, as the writer of the *Tao-Te-Ching* astutely noted. What we desire is to make those opposites so firmly entrenched and concrete that nothing gets defined outside of a rather solid perspective. This works especially well with the notion of male-female because after all this time they still remain total mysteries to one another. Often they define themselves in total opposition to, if not isolation from, each other. This means they generally end up absolutely conflicted about how to relate.

Their inability to see the deeper unity of being human brings them much pain and misery. By not seeing other human beings as part of themselves, they end up estranged from one another, and there are few things we like more than alienation and estrangement. It is the breeding ground for so many more emotions and perceived slights that bring them closer to us.

But more than their personal relationships, it is in their political orders that we seek to enhance this notion of the opposite, the other, the separate. We enjoy it when they divide themselves into two warring camps. One of them once said that politics is the art of dividing people from one another. I even heard one of them say that politics was of the devil. Out of the mouths of babes, huh?

When handled skillfully—and we seem to be in total and absolute control of this one these days—they end up defining themselves in opposition to one another rather than celebrating their common humanity or working on the problems they face together. If we play our cards right, this usually ends up badly for them, happily for us, much like the guns-and-knives mentality that presently exists among them. All this is very satisfying, and, I must say, politics has been wildly successful at keeping them from embracing one another in the way our enemy desires.

POSTED BY BLZBB AT 12:34 AM, 25/04
TAGS: DEMOCRATS | REPUBLICANS | TORIES | LABOR | BHARATIYA JANATA PARTY | INDIAN NATIONAL CONGRESS PARTY | ETC., ETC.

# Separate, but Certainly Not Equal

Continuing a theme from upstairs, I want to take a minute and reflect some more on opposites. The first step is separation. We want to separate everything. We want to separate their home from their work; we want to separate their families from one another; we want to separate the public from the private. We want to drive wedges between all aspects of their lives that were at one time unified.

If we keep the separations in place, even in the heart of their politics, we nurture the divide-and-conquer mentality that always works in our favor. One way this benefits us is by them engineering the divisions to be so strong, with enough implicit violence, that the only thing that can save them is the state. It is the state that possesses the power they should have within themselves. In many of their communities, it is the state that will be able to regulate them, keep them in line, protect them from one another. In this way, the modern state becomes the most omnipotent institution in their lives, far more important than church, synagogue, or mosque.

The more we can separate them, the more space we occupy, because we inhabit the empty spaces anyway. But as I have insistently been telling you throughout this blog, we are well served by the separations they bring into their lives. We want them to prize their vaunted individuality so much that they lose sight of a larger community of concerns, even if that community is their own partner. If they stroke their egos to the point that they cannot accept any other claim on life other than their own selves, then their own selfishness will eventually destroy them. We want to see each person clinging to their own life like a two-year-old grasping a toy, yelling, "Mine! Mine! Mine!"

POSTED BY BLZBB AT 4:56 AM, 26/04
TAGS: TERRIBLE TWOS

# Respect My Authoritah!

Colleagues, part of our success has been ensuring that whatever desires and hopes our rival has for these creatures does not even factor into their decisions about how to live their lives. If we put their desire for "god" into the category of the irrational and superstitious, then it is easy for them to discount the claim that our foe has any desires for them.

Remember earlier when I said that they stopped being concerned about how to build relationships among themselves and became fixated on how to manage their lives effectively? Well, if that is the case, then forget the notion of moral convictions; there is nothing remotely connected to our rival that guides them for the most part. Oh, there is an eruption of graced living here and there, but these are few and far between.

They only have themselves to blame, of course. Looking at the empirical evidence in front of them, they came to the only logical conclusion that they could about what type of creatures they are. Humans are depraved, some of them argued, and nothing is going to help them. Hard to see how they could come to any other conclusion, given all the facts.

So, where they saw (and some still see) only sin, we saw enormous possibilities and potential for constructing our company in their midst. And, truly, what exists today in their public spaces that speaks of, or manifests, the perspective of our opponent? We get them to build entire structures around the idea of justice, but unless that is tempered by mercy, what do they get? Well, the answer is self-evident, isn't it? They get the hard demands of justice alone.

They have nowhere else to go at this point. They cannot go back in time to push the reset button and start all over again, and going forward on the path they are on just means they continue in the same well-worn tracks that have served us so well over the years. We want the nasty, short, and brutish. I'm actually mystified by what our enemy wants.

I know virtue, goodness, and flourishing rest at the heart of what our enemy desires, but then why give them the will to make decisions and choices? We find it better to compel people to do what we want. Compulsion, coercion and control, surveillance and order, these are the work of our hands. Structuring them along these lines has been a tried and tested way of giving them what they need—structure. Authority must be respected, after all, don't you think?

Our opponent seeks to subvert us every bit as much as we seek to subvert what "god" wants to manifest among them. Don't ever forget this. There is no negotiation, no middle ground, no letting up. To keep them in line, they must respect our authority.

POSTED BY BLZBB AT 7:30 AM, 28/04

TAGS: ERIC CARTMAN  |  *SOUTH PARK*  |  ORIGINAL SIN

..........................................................................................................

## Will It Go 'Round in Circles?

Destruction is the very background hum of being in their lives; it surrounds them with a slight buzzing, always on the edge, waiting for the right moment to be called onto the scene. How does this happen?

Well, sometimes it happens like this: the theme of victimhood get picked up and carried forward through their media (see above) and other information-spreading institutions, rumors are spread, stories get told, narratives are built. Nuanced at first, the virus takes hold as the cacophony builds. Suddenly the person who sees life differently from me is more than someone whom I cannot understand. Now they become the "beast" that threatens my very survival.

Songs are written, plays are staged, pictures are painted, rallies are held, flags are unfurled, and we take up residence. Those who do not join the dance of madness are ostracized, cast out, believed to be pollutions to purity. Soon someone makes the eminently sensible suggestion: "Something must be done about X." Quickly, solutions are offered, and if we are fortunate enough someone proposes a way to deal with "the problem" once and for all. Of course, this solution will resolve "the problem" by cleansing the stain from their midst. If we are really lucky, they will go for the "Final Solution."

They shape reality in such a way that their very survival rests under the umbrella of violence and destruction we provide. We colonize their hearts by shaping them so adroitly they will never even have the social imagination to realize another way exists for them to live. They often want to do the right thing, but they cannot bring themselves to, you know, actually do it.

It never occurs to the majority of them that they should hate their hatred, despise their condescension, resist all the habits that prepare the way for violence to be unleashed into the world. Once you take away their imagination to think about how the world should go and lock them into what is *real*, it becomes pretty easy to just sit back and watch the carnage.

They become the air we breathe, the water we drink, and the bread of our sustenance. If we will live, we must come and feed. Their inability to resist the soft seductions of victimhood or the hard seductions of power keeps us alive. Things that they would never consider doing as individuals become plausible under the authority of a system or an institution like government.

Their inability to let someone different inhabit their world provides fresh soil for evil to grow. Their inability to resist the feelings and emotions that result from their undeserved suffering allows us to plant the most toxic seeds of destruction.

POSTED BY BLZBB AT 1:20 AM, 30/04

TAGS: FINAL SOLUTION | NATIONALISM | ARISTOCENTRISM | BILLY PRESTON, "WILL IT GO 'ROUND IN CIRCLES?"

## Spread All Over the World—One-Quarter of an Inch Deep

Mass media has become extraordinary useful to our cause. In truth, I can say that if it weren't for the media we would not have been able to have as much success as we have had in the world. The media push our agenda in so many ways it amazes me sometimes. For instance, take their endless fascination with the theatrical aspects of the modern world. They build a cult of personality around individuals and then turn everything into a personal food fight. Since this is the only way they can conceptualize anything at all, they seldom get to the point where they actually ask questions about the type of world they are building.

Something only matters to them if the propa . . . excuse me, news media, chum it out for consumption. No communal struggling with the shadows that plague their lives, only obsession about who's up and who's down, who's winning, who's losing, really superficial stuff. We appreciate their focus on the mundane and superficial because it pulls them deeper into creatures who have lost the ability to think clearly and wisely about the world they are building.

We want them to obsess over the minute and petty, the up-to-date and that which is right in front of them. If we can get them to define themselves by the immediate distractions, they lose sight of the things that could tear them from our loving embrace. We especially don't want them thinking about our opponent in any other way than what we desire.

Some of them believe so much in their politics that political life becomes the only way they can understand themselves. Any other path to meaning in their lives is closed off by attention to the latest political fight or celebrity. Nothing substantial allows them the full consideration of their decisions. The cultivation of different ways of life, or even the necessity of occasional solitude, is little known among them. I love it when they have a constant noise in their ears; it keeps them from facing themselves.

POSTED BY BLZBB AT **4:29 AM, 02/05**
TAGS: **RUPERT MURDOCH** | **FOX NEWS** | **BRITISH SKY BROADCASTING** | **GENERAL ELECTRIC** | **CELL PHONES** | **IPODS**

......................................................................................

# She Blinded Me with Science

There has been some discussion in the comments lately about science and religion. Some of you seem quite excited about the prospects for continuing disillusionment by the use of science to discredit any of the narratives they believe about religion.

Of course, this has always been one of the benefits of science, but you have to be careful here because science is a double-edged sword. In one respect, their pursuit of science is just a way of gathering knowledge about themselves and the world they live within. In that regard, it is a gift given to them in their innate curiosity.

This proclivity in them has given them much: longer lives, better health, baseball at a distance, Hubble telescope pictures, coffee makers, and so much more. These are the type of things they could not have without science and technology. As such, science is not much use to us at all. In fact, it annoys me how they are able to make it work for them as much as they do.

But it is when science moves into the area of ideology that I find it useful. As ideology, science becomes the absolute and sole authority to define their lives. Nothing is regarded as true unless it can be proven, and proof is only what science says it is. Well, now, we can get somewhere with this. If we push all meaning and truth in their lives into this narrow peninsula of thinking, we can take more space for ourselves.

Along this path, science becomes authoritarian and effectively shuts down all dissent. This is something we love, the silencing of all alternatives. Anyone who launches a critique on science today runs the risk of total and absolute ridicule, even when that critic is sometimes right. Often what the critic is criticizing is a particular ordering of science that seeks to exhaust all meaning in its particular interpretations of the universe.

Take the issue of materialism, for example. Remember when I first started this blog I said that one thing that is crucial for us to keep from them as much as possible is that matter contains so much more than they even realize; indeed, matter contains the very life of our enemy within it. But who today really believes that, except for the granola-eating, Birkenstock-wearing, crystal-gazing crunchies who spend all their time waving music out of their eyes at Phish concerts? We want to make sure that "god" is dematerialized in every possible way.

We want their science to convince them that all meaning, all value, all worth exhausts itself in the world of matter. Materialism is a useful doctrine because many will defend it with the passion of a fundamentalist. Its power becomes absolute in the modern world because it and it alone has the preeminent power of explanation. What defines for many of them what is rational and what is not? It is the particular interpretations that science gives them.

You see, what has happened is that science has become something more than a tool to explore the world and make their lives better, it has become a regime of power that cannot under any circumstances be called into question as the dominant authority because that would be, well, just stupid.

What is stupid is that some of them are unable to separate the ideological uses of science from science itself. After all, look at where we are with them and their science. Sure, we have all that stuff we hate, the stuff that enhances their lives, makes their lives easier, feeds and clothes, even heals them. But as we mentioned before, they have used their knowledge to establish more control, surveillance, and destructive power. The fact that they might need to cultivate spiritual disciplines to use all this power never occurs to them.

POSTED BY BLZBB AT 8:12 AM, 03/05
TAGS: **THOMAS DOLBY** | **RICHARD DAWKINS** | **PHISH** | **W. V. QUINE**

......................................................................................................

## It's Not Really War, but We Want Them to Believe It Is

In response to my last post I got the following message:

*I understand what you are saying about the ideological uses of science and all, but, and please don't eat me for this, it does give them truth, and didn't you say we hate truth almost as much as we hate love? I understand your pleasure in something like the war between science and religion, and the way we can twist the truth to rest only on the science side of the issue, but I am not sure I see where we should be so confident in science to construct a world to our liking.*

Okay, this one time you don't go on the barbeque, but why don't you get this? Our whole game is getting them to use the things that are gifts from our enemy in ways that create space for us to colonize their lives and eventually make ourselves comfortable in their home. This is one way science has been as helpful as religion has been.

If one wants to be respectable in their world, one must be scientific about things. All discourse that science does not control becomes seen as suspect because it cannot be empirically based. When science is the first-order means of knowing all things, then all other ways of knowing the world become secondary and easily dismissed.

The poet can no longer give them any truth (other than what they create); the writer can no longer reveal something profoundly and deeply true because it cannot be quantified. But science gives them the *real* world, or at least this is what we hope they think. Many of them think that science's truths are deeper than the poet's, when in reality it is actually the other way around.

Science has been with them from the beginning. From the moment their consciousness developed the ability to examine, make judgments, and assess the world they are embedded within, science has been a necessary companion. The ancient philosophers were certainly no strangers to science. Remember all that time Aristotle spent looking at tide pools? The ancients were no less curious than the present-day creatures are. Of course, the beauty, even back then, was that they would use their knowledge to build better weapons.

It is this use they put to things that we want to leverage. It neither helps nor harms us when they peer into their microscopes, or gaze into their telescopes, or even discover things they had never known before. We find their joy at discovery can be somewhat irritating, but that is a small price to pay for the glorious results of their sciences. Because when that first stick becomes a catapult, when that first spark becomes gunpowder, when that first spear point becomes a bullet? Well, this just testifies to our ability to take space in their world.

See what happens when science becomes the absolute ideology? It takes the provisional and turns it into the universal. When they take some transitory interpretation of existence and raise it to the level of an absolute, inviolate, and practically sacred universal idea that *must* be accepted because science says so, we are amused. Who doesn't take the *law* of gravity seriously? Taking boundary conditions like gravity, though, and then assuming that all reality is material confuses what might *really* be the most important thing.

This habit of mind is fun because it works with both science and religion. This can be subtle, but close to the same thing. Once you slip into seeing reality in a set way, it becomes difficult to dislodge that particular perspective. Even though they know data are theory laden, they invest an idea or discovery with absolute authority and it becomes difficult to dispel. Indeed, any attack on the idea itself becomes a threat.

Depending on what authority has the most social power, that is the view that gets accepted. Over the years, science has shown itself to be far more pragmatically reliable than the revelation of their religions or even their poets. Testable hypotheses, public verification, repeatable results in testing—all those elements of scientific method become so much easier to trust than some religious story from long ago. The results of centuries of science carry so much weight among them that it becomes difficult to really question things that they believe science has "settled."

This picture of what has been "settled" represents a masterpiece for our purposes. Everything is matter and nothing but matter. They grasp the particles whizzing into and out of existence, they dimly perceive strange attractors, they discover Fibonacci sequences, or Feigenbaum constants, yet often their interpretation of these phenomena offers only one possibility. All the amazing behaviors of natural systems are totally the results of time, chance, and randomness. You would think the underlying mathematical elegance of things might lead them to think about other possibilities, but nope, for some of them science has closed off that road. It never occurs to ask why the universe shows such intricate patterning if it is totally random. Even to entertain that it is consciousness all down the line is a bridge too far for some of them to cross.

POSTED BY BLZBB AT 10:39 PM, 05/05
TAGS: FIBONACCI SEQUENCES | DISCOVERY CHANNEL TELESCOPE | THOMAS KUHN, *THE STRUCTURE OF SCIENTIFIC REVOLUTIONS*

........................................................................................

## Intelligent Design?

In my last entry, I left off with the notion of chance and order, which for us is not a big deal; we see it around here all the time. If anyone knows the implications of that, our realm does. But what I was trying to point out to you was how fascinating it is when they finally get to this stage and then the fundamentalists on both sides simply miss the point.

Those on the religious side see the underlying mathematical elegance and build an ideology like intelligent design and then construct their images of our enemy in such a way that any other truths get lost to them. Do you remember my earlier statements about how they construct their image of "god" around a certain way of understanding metaphysics? They can't help themselves, and their religions function as a tool in their desire to combat what they think is a threat to their world. Science itself is not their enemy, but they seem confused about this.

The fundamentalists on the science side of this continuum are the mirror image in some ways. They tend to ignore the evidence of the structure and pay attention to the random. In this they make some significant leaps in logic to argue against the notion of anything like an implicit order in the cosmos.

I am especially enamored of their creative use of the term "promissory materialism." Given enough time and knowledge, they argue, they will be able to prove that everything is sufficiently explained by materialism. The beautiful part of this is that if you assume material explanations going in, you are likely to find what you are looking for. Data tend to be theory laden, so they will end up interpreting the data in ways that confirm their previous ideas. It works that way for everyone.

Take something like consciousness, which defies all their abilities to define it because it emerges from the unfolding of the universe in new and novel ways that cannot be contained in their theories. They proclaim that one day they will unlock the mysteries of free will on the basis of the chemical and neural processes of the brain. Or, perhaps they will convince themselves there is no such thing as will. Good luck with that. How much more faithful could you get than promissory materialism? Everything will be explained, all mysteries will be solved, but only if people believe and have faith in the way that has been predetermined by science. The only interpretation that will be allowed is one that holds open the possibility of future explanation. "god"-of-the-gaps, meet science-of-the-just-give-us-some-more-time.

You see how "faithful" both sides are? They each believe in what their empirical observations tell them, but then they construct oppositional ideologies that distort both science and religion. Given the evidence available to them both, one side comes out with intelligent design; the other side comes out with intelligent chance (you just can't ignore the numbers is all I'm saying). But that they come out incomprehensible to one another is what we love. We always appreciate confusion. It's even better when they throw in contempt for one another.

POSTED BY BLZBB AT 7:45 PM, 07/05

TAGS: STUART HAMEROFF  |  THE DISCOVERY INSTITUTE  |  RICHARD DAWKINS  |  WILLIAM DEMBSKI  |  DAVID BOHM

## The Devil Went Down to Dover

I feel as if I should keep on with our present topic, and I have one quick observation to make. Given what I have already said, doesn't it strike you as a confirmation of what I am arguing that some of the most religious among them argue their case on the basis of science? The religious fundamentalists have accepted science's ability to control the narrative of who they are to the extent that all truth must be scientific truth, even for them.

Take, for example, their creation stories. In the first writings of some of the early tribes, especially the ones where I play the starring role and get them to go against "god's" wishes, there are some accounts that tell the story in a certain way. Our enemy creates the earth and all existence emerges from the desire to create. Pretty much a story that speaks to the relationship that matter has to "god." I hate this story, except the part in the second telling where my wisdom is on full display (*Did "god" really say . . . ?*).

The stories themselves emerge from particular historical circumstances when the Jews were trying to define themselves over against the culture of Babylon, which had just taken them captive. Thus, they portrayed an image of "god" that addresses how to create without violence (unlike, say, the Babylonian stories of the *Enuma Elish*). The stories exist as a narrative rendering of the relationship between "god" and one particular set of humans.

But notice how some on the religious end feel the need to prove the stories are scientifically accurate and argue on the basis of science for their authority. These creatures sometimes even lack the imagination to realize that some things don't have to be scientifically accurate to be true. But because of the hegemony of science, truth can only exist in a scientific form. I am not sure why the most devout often look to science to validate their religious belief, but when they argue on the basis of science for the truth of their narratives, it is really unnecessary.

Do you see what I have been trying to say? Even those who are absolutely opposed to science and its interpretations argue their case on the authority of science. They are doomed before they begin, because once you accept your opponent's premises you have lost the argument.

This is one reason why we should not concede an inch to our opponent. "god" believes that they will somehow be able to respond to the light that they are immersed in. I think exactly the opposite and, seriously, when you take a look at things as they presently stand, who has the better of it?

POSTED BY BLZBB AT 1:21 AM, 08/05

TAGS: **BABYLONIAN CAPTIVITY** | *ENUMA ELISH* | **TIAMAT** | **MARDUK** | *KITZMILLER V. DOVER* | **THE DISCOVERY INSTITUTE**

# The Homecoming

Continuing on in what has become a thread of interest to many of you, but for what reason I can't figure out, I have some other observations to make. Some of you seem most interested in evolution and its potential to destroy faith. I think you confuse categories here. Sure, that particular narrative itself has assumed a powerful role in shaping how they view the world. Sometimes it even leads to interesting philosophical positions that are to our liking. But you should be careful. It is a particular interpretation of matter that allows us space.

You know as well as I do that as the universe began its journey to existence, as atoms began to form from subatomic particles, as the very matrix of forces that allow for life to emerge came into being, this was beyond spectacular. Even we have to grant that one. The dance of energy and matter that went on between mass-carrying electrons, protons, and neutrons forming quarks, atoms capturing electrons, was truly a singular moment.

We are aware of the self-organization that emerged in this whirling fandango. Our access to knowledge is no less than theirs on this account, though our experience of things may be a bit deeper. Anyway, back to the nightmare. This collision of everything released energies into the world and formed planets, suns, and emptiness. I never suspected the creative cunning that rested at the heart of all this.

Who could have foreseen among this chaos the emergence of cells, organisms, DNA, strings of biological life that would stagger like a newborn colt finding its legs to take its place among all the energies present? From the beginnings of a ball of gas, a world of such rich complexity and, I hate using this word, beauty appeared.

Novelty upon novelty emerged as gases formed and condensed into galaxies. What one story could have held all that?

The story that science gives them is not a bad one. In fact, as long as they keep in front of them the realization that what they know today may need to be reevaluated in the future, they will continue to find out new things they do not yet suspect. But science will never be able to show them the spirit of matter. I prefer it when they are convinced that matter is empty, devoid of spirit because spirit is a thing that cannot be measured or quantified. It is even better if they think the word *spirit* sounds spooky, superstitious.

We want to ensure that type of knowledge never becomes an aspect of science. No, a science that is able to intuit spirit should never become a part of their world. We want those who fight so hard to protect science's hegemony in the modern world to remain the dominant voices. We like the illusions of objectivity they cling to, because it diminishes any other possible truth.

This way, when someone probes why the universe develops through such complexity and self-organization, they are only allowed one answer. If the question is why the universe operates in such a way that life is possible, we really only want one option—that's just the way it is. Because, when you think about it, what other answer could their science give?

POSTED BY BLZBB AT 3:49 AM, 09/05
TAGS: **SELF-ORGANIZING SYSTEMS | TELEOLOGY**

...................................................................................................

# All Things Bright and Beautiful

I want to make sure you focus their attention on some of the problems inherent in this process. We have taken much ground over the years when they ask questions like, "Why would 'god' create a world where predation is how things survive? Why is there so much suffering built into life?"

We appreciate it when they keep their mind focused on the problems with the way things are. Any fool can be convinced when they look at nature that it is "red in tooth and claw." I take special delight in this aspect of the natural order. Since destruction is the coin of our realm, keep them focused on that.

Bring to their attention bugs that inject their prey with enzymes, paralyzing them while all life is sucked out of their latest lunch. With that one bite, the victim's muscles, bones, and organs dissolve under the influence of that poison. Talk about a Happy Meal; we ourselves cannot do much better than that.

These examples can be multiplied; shoot, just get them hooked on Animal Planet. Most of that is like watching lunchtime around here anyway. But you get the point. Focus their attention on the waste and unnecessary suffering found in the world. Point out the odd arrangements, the inchoate violence found in the very fabric of the cosmos. There are numerous examples of viruses, galaxies exploding, snow leopards chasing hares, lions chasing springboks available for consideration. You get the point.

It is not very far from asking these questions, or just pointing out the reality in front of them, that one can start asking the questions that really plant the seeds we want to water. Oh, sure, they'll get in their campers and go visit the park, or they will walk the savannah and watch the sunset thinking to themselves how beautiful it all is, but soon enough we want to turn their attention to what is right in front of them—nature is one vast killing field.

Look, here, another carcass where the strong took its prey; look, there, another animal viciously and efficiently mangled by a creature in search of filling an empty stomach. Have them think about why the universe gives them bore worms that burrow into a host's body to lay their eggs while they feed on the host's blood. They should be thinking about poisons that kill upon contact and viruses that kill indiscriminately. We want them to be terrified of the disease that dissolves the body and leaves the deflated balloon that used to house a human being. All things bright and beautiful, huh?

I could go all day letting these delicious examples roll off my tongue (which really does look a lot like Gene Simmons's), but the main issue is to keep them asking how a "god" of love could have created a world of such cunning destruction. How is it that we see so much waste and suffering in the world? If "god" is omnipotent, wouldn't the world look very different?

The experts in the matter, the scientists, come in and say that yes, the universe we can observe with our own two eyes (never mind all those fabulous instruments we have), has the form one should expect of no design, no purpose, no good, no evil, just pointless violence and randomness. Like shooting fish in a barrel, actually, which reminds me, let's break for lunch.

POSTED BY BLZBB 11:54 AM, 10/05
TAGS: SURVIVAL OF THE FITTEST | NATURAL SELECTION | GIANT WATER BUG | ANNIE DILLARD, *PILGRIM AT TINKER CREEK*

........................................................................................................

# They're All Just Trapped in an Ingmar Bergman Movie

Okay, all that talk of prey and eating made me hungry. Anyway, back to the issue at hand. This is one way of spreading the doubts that we can use later in taking them to despair. For all of their romanticizing nature, many of them live in a world where they are remarkably unfamiliar with death. It is a part of existence, but they refuse the ubiquity. Others are more than acquainted with death; they see so much of it they have just come to expect what we point out to the others. Curiously enough, the more they truly grasp and make their peace with death; the less they seem to fear it.

We don't want them to see that in some ways their life is a pilgrimage to death, that the entire cosmic dance of life contains death. We want them terrified of death. We want death to appear random and scary and something to be feared (see Fear, Inc.), not something that is a natural part of the journey. We also don't want them to see that death is not quite the ending they have envisioned, because as we know very well, new life always comes from the death of other things. It is one of the mysteries that perplexes us.

But our main concern is to keep up the confusion among them about the world they can observe and the beliefs they have about our opponent. Statements about the shape of the world and why "god" allows it to be the way it is do two things. It hides their responsibility for what goes in their part of the universe, and it gives them another false image of "god" to struggle with.

For centuries, most of them have envisioned "god" as something so far beyond them spatially that they cannot even begin to conceive that something is intimately at work in life. That the life of our enemy could be so embedded within the ongoing life and death of the world, that our rival shares every moment of existence, the suffering, the death, the vulnerability of it all—well, it is just too much for them.

They have grown up thinking that "god" is something removed from the world, something that acts upon the world, but certainly not immersed within it or vulnerable to it in any way. They cannot imagine, because they have little experience with this type of imagination, that "god" shares every moment of existence. Nothing is outside "god," but "god" infuses all life, experiencing simply everything.

Certainly their narratives of the creative aspects of "god" didn't prepare them for this. I referenced those stories before, but it was the cultural reception of the first stories and the images of "god" which they portrayed that have had such an impact in solidifying the image in their minds. We want them to see our opponent as the cosmic Santa Claus, removed from the earth, in some place inaccessible, and keeping the cosmic records of who gets what at the end. It always surprises me how widespread this image is, even among their most thoughtful and educated.

In their ancient stories, "god" created all this and stands back, removed from the action, and to suggest otherwise means that the creator becomes the creation. I'll tell you something else, colleagues: creation, in their minds, is a once-and-for-all action of the past. They never suspect that creation is an ongoing process that brings forth new forms of life. They never grasp that the ongoing dance of life is nourished by the spirit of our enemy and is something we fight daily and try our best to destroy.

In the world of constant becoming, "god" is in, with, and under these unfolding processes of life. This is why we cannot rest for one moment, because our rival never rests in working with creation, nourishing it with information, suggestions, and spirit. I swear I won't rest until I see this all gone in a wisp of smoke.

In reality, creativity is our enemy's desire at work. The action of creating continues and is always ongoing. The creation continues on and in some mysterious way brings forth new life from the death of the old. This seems to be an ongoing part of "god's" very existence. I don't understand it myself, but our enemy even participates in death.

They do not see their suffering as having a point, and we must keep it this way. I want to make sure they never see the dance of life as redemptive. I actually rather like some of the newer stories they create and tell one another. The thought that life is driven by the pursuit of the selfish need to survive and flourish sort of mimics what our opponent has in mind, but in their telling of the tale, they miss the point.

Part of our success is found right here. Who among them even thinks in terms of suffering for the redemption of life? Who really conceives that "god" desires relationship with *all* of creation in its coming to be? First of all, it just sounds stupid to the ears of modernity, doesn't it? This is absolutely not an interpretation that anyone even considers worth talking about. Certainly science is not going to allow such a preposterous story a role in interpreting the world.

No one considers that the life of "god" might be found in the immense suffering of the world. It is implausible to think "god" is immersed in the processes of life, not only creating the potentialities of life, but rooted within them, struggling with and responding to their choices. You can't put that on a stained-glass window like you can a bearded guy on a throne. Few consider that our rival has this experience, this vulnerability. That one-sided remote transcendence of tradition is something they can more easily grasp, and we are the better for it.

The gulf between the mystery of the universe, a cosmos infused with purpose, and the everyday life they live is so great that it cannot be bridged by most of them. The reality of "god" is now so remote and closed off from their everyday life as to be meaningless. Sure, they struggle with the mystery of it all, don't they, but do you think they often rise to entertain the thought that the universe moves toward something? It is an adventure they don't even realize they are on most of the time.

POSTED BY BLZBB AT 2:34 PM, 10/05

TAGS: DEATH | DIVINE VULNERABILITY | INGMAR BERGMAN, *THE SEVENTH SEAL*

# Benevolence?

It is hard for them to conceive, isn't it? I have been sharing with you my take on the great mystery of existence, and this has some of you anxious. The god of metaphysical abstraction is a far more comfortable image than the one I am showing you. If it makes you nervous, just think how it makes them feel upon first hearing that everything they thought was true and solid is not as solid as they think it is. There is quite the gap between the image and the reality, but this is true with simply everything, as their philosophers have always pointed out to them. Faith is lived out between the spaces of belief and doubt, but we want them to think it dwells in rock-hard certainty.

A bit more about the universe, however, before we leave this topic and move onto other things. It is important for us when they sow the seeds of confusion and doubt. I laid out for you earlier how easy this is when we look at the world itself. If there is a designer here, it is hard to see. In fact, the case can be made that "god" is nothing more than a sadistic monster who enjoys the ripping beak, the sharp tooth sinking into flesh, the toxin finding its prey. I myself have made this case, not only here, but elsewhere as well. I am quite proud of pointing out the obvious to anyone who will lend me an ear.

Frankly, I am at a loss to understand how anyone could not see it my way, truth be told. It seems so evident. This is why we love the intelligent-design folks so much. They do grasp the math, you have to give them that. They see the order behind the whole thing, but they have a larger problem because once you say there is a designer at work, the difficult nature of things kind of pops out, doesn't it?

We come along with our questions and logic and raise the issues. "How is it that a benevolent 'god' could create such a world as we see around us?" Point out to them the numerous examples of senseless destruction and mindless waste and then watch how that intelligent-design thing works out for them. The pressure that the facts exert has to turn them away from any other explanation that doesn't seem like whistling in the graveyard. Sometimes they resort to the notion that the earth shares in the fall from grace, but this is pretty thin stuff, if you ask me.

This is why the secular turn has so enriched our lives. Once they no longer think in any way that is remotely theological, they are on our territory. In this day and age, who would even consider that life is one constant state of divine becoming? It is hard to accept that the life of "god" is found in all its potentialities, its unfolding beauty, even in its suffering. It is precisely in the suffering where new and novel possibilities emerge in the death of what has gone before.

No one sees what we do, colleagues. This is another thing we hate. The world in all its coming to be is informed with the spirit of suffering love, a suffering that participates in the contradictions of life, a suffering that brings new life out of death, a suffering that at its heart reveals the inexhaustive creative power of love to make a home in the world. Death and resurrection is not a once-and-for-all action, but a continuing movement of desire.

The mystery that we see and want to keep hidden from them is that underneath it all is the very eros of our despised and hated foe. Life itself is a passion play. It makes me queasy inside to consider where this is all going. We must make sure that we keep them from this realization, because if they were to leave the comfortable worlds of their cultural constructs, they might see the exquisite beauty of the mundane. I hate them sometimes, almost as much as I envy them.

POSTED BY BLZBB AT 2:39 AM, 13/05

TAGS: **RESURRECTION** | **PLATO** | **CAVES** | **HOLMES ROLSTON III**

# Rumors of Glory

They have shaped their consciousnesses around the way a story gets told all of their pathetic lives. Most of those stories shape them in ways we appreciate (see, for example, Progress), but some stories hold truths that create problems for us. Since we are dealing with primal stories, just a couple of thoughts for you today. The narrative most of the followers of the BODY accept is the one where there was an original perfection in the past that was lost. We've mentioned this previously.

I like this framing of the story quite a bit because it keeps them thinking that their goal rests in a past they can never attain. If they think their lives are marred by the loss of perfection and innocence, then the present represents for them an exile from the garden. This gives them a view of their "nature" that benefits us. When the violence, betrayal, and selfishness they are prone to manifests itself, they can always just fall back on the tried and true, "Oh well, we're human. What are you going to do?" There's plenty they could do, but they won't. They suspect that something is wrong, perhaps desperately distorted, given the way they act, but this is a vague and illusive thing in their minds. They have therapists for that now.

Other thinkers have seen different ways to interpret those primal narratives, but these people have never become the dominant voices in their culture. One of their ancients, Irenaeus, thought that they were created with the potential for perfection. He believed the goal of their lives was divinization, of conforming to our enemy. They were created as creatures of mud destined to become divine themselves. Seriously, who would believe such a thing as that? It sounds absolutely ridiculous given the evidence.

As long as the practical atheism of the modern world holds prominence, we can count on the fact that no alternative story to the one that they have believed for millennia will shape their consciousness. We can rest assured that they will never embrace a story that sees perfection as a future goal. We want their life to be exile from the garden, not journey and quest toward a different and better destiny. True home for them must be ever out of reach in the past. We especially don't want them to see home as a promise forgotten, resting in the future, awaiting their embrace. Or, if they do, then we must make perfection an absolute ideal that they believe they can reach on their own steam. As mentioned before, the desire for perfection can be like the desire for purity, and in our hands both these have been good weapons to use. No, the type of perfection we don't want them to consider is that of hope

If they start to think in terms of promise and hope, then we lose space, ground gets taken that is hard to win back. Suffering itself becomes defined differently for them. Just as it is our rival's capacity for suffering that sustains the natural order, it is their capacity for seeing suffering as participation in "god's" life that threatens to undo all our hard work.

Having felt the depth of suffering, they sometimes become aware of "god's" presence. When they refuse to flee suffering, they become resistant to us, and we hate this. I really wish I didn't have to lay this out because it makes me uncomfortable, but when some of them experience the depths of "god's" suffering, they resist more intently all the forms of violence and deceit that bring suffering to their world.

Their deep grasp of suffering leads some of them to resist the claims of allegiance that social and political constructions make upon them. They move beyond the absolute claims society or culture command. These claims are usually the types of demands that will lead them to war with one another. There are those who act out of a different story, and it frustrates me that we cannot easily pull them into the dichotomies of Us/Them. In their refusal to bow the knee to the penultimate, they destabilize us and lessen our presence among them.

The ones who actually believe that the hope of a new creation is possible all too often end up slipping from our clutches. We prefer them to think of the future in apocalyptic terms. We don't want them to embrace the future as a space where the life of our enemy fills the territory we claim as our own. It is in their willingness to endure suffering so that redemption might be manifest that we face our greatest challenge. We've been through that before, and I am here to tell you, that did not go well for us. When I think of the BODY I still get the shivers.

If they are going to insist on the idea that "god" creates the world, it is better when they conceive of creation as a once-and-done event. That way, we can keep them focused on the arrow of history, moving to the consummation, always apocalyptic, always with violence. I have already pointed out to you that the book of Revelation itself says that the kingdom of heaven suffers violence, and the violent will take it by force. Of all their sacred texts, this one has given me the most hope that we are not working in vain. If we can create enough violence in the world, we may, in fact, take our rightful place, not only on earth, but also in heaven.

POSTED BY BLZBB AT 6:23 AM, 14/05
TAGS: IRENAEUS OF LYONS

..........................................................................................

# Pacing the Cage

The dominant orders that they have established provide such a comfortable home for us today. We do see them struggling against the attitudes, practices, and values that ensure their destruction. Envy, rage, jealously, revenge, and so much more constitute the prisons of their lives. Sometimes I wonder if they are in love with their own destruction.

Occasionally, one of them understands the cage, sees that the way out rests in leaving the prisons of resentment and oppression and greed they have built in the heart of their politics and economics. Then they no longer root their identity in the powers they live under. This threatens our very existence. They are harder to nudge when they disconnect like that.

When they stop pacing the cage, when they step out of it, they don't behave like a victim seeking revenge. They are no longer imprisoned within the memory of a thousand injustices. They slip inexorably from our grasp. Their vision has expanded and their hearts have been enlarged by something alien to us. They detach themselves from the reality that they are creating to discover a new life, and often that life will resist the orders we desperately wish they would give their unquestioning allegiance.

We simply do not have the ability to grasp how they can go over to the BODY and love the enemy. The willingness to see the enemy as worthy of regard or consideration is absolute nihilism to my mind. Compassion must never be allowed to flourish among them. We must never stop our efforts to marginalize such people as foolish, naive, dangerous, and, frankly, suicidal.

POSTED BY BLZBB AT 1:23 PM, 15/05

TAGS: **MAX WEBER** | **CAGES** | **NEO** | *THE MATRIX*

# Mad Men

Do you remember that charming and delightful story of Nietzsche regarding his madman? Rushing into the public square, the madman mourns the loss of "god." He goes back and forth in the square calling with an anguished voice that "god" is dead, and they have killed him. He provokes derision and laughter from those present. "Is He hidden?" some ask. "Has He gotten lost?" others inquire. All the questions of their mockery surround the madman, but he stops at one point and lays it all out for them.

"Where is god?" he asks. Why, "god" has been murdered and everyone present to the madman's voice helped to pull the trigger, plant the knife, twist the rope. The madman goes on to paint a picture of a world without "god," and it isn't pretty. The world is shifting on its axis, the oceans are soaked up by a huge sponge, day becomes night, night becomes day. Nothing is the same, and everything is so much worse than it was before. In frustration, the madman takes the lantern in his hand and smashes it on the ground. Up to this point, I have always loved this story if for no other reason than it shows how much real estate we have acquired.

And here the story takes a really interesting turn: the madman looks at his mocking audience and proclaims he has come too early, that his time is not yet. In fact, he tells his hearers, the true horrific nature of the news that he brings has not arrived in full force. Like light coming from a distant star, the reality of the moment they are all living in has not totally arrived. They do not yet realize the truth of the madman's proclamation. They do not even realize that they have committed deicide.

I have been telling you, colleagues, a tale that points to the truth of this story. Everything, simply everything that presently drives much

of their world, is done now on the basis of the absence of "god."
What is even better, from our perspective, is that the gods they do
create in their religions to justify their orders are locked in violent
struggle with one another. Many of them think that the other's deity
is a threat to their worlds. They may be right.

They have no sight for where they should be moving. They see no
direction that guides them, no pull toward something holy. There
is no eros seeking, pleading, calling, luring them to a better future.
Now they go on their own steam, but as they move into the future
they do not realize that "god" is dead in any recognizable way to
them. Many of their societies are constructed on the assumption
that "god" has no real voice in the matter. And the ones that do
construct themselves on what they believe about "god" scare the
crap out of the rest of them.

"god" just doesn't figure into a plausible world for so many of
those who call the shots. What is considered plausible, what seems
workable, is what holds the most attraction for them, and this
focuses their efforts. The world has become vacated of any other
considerations save the practical ones, and this pleases me. I am
happy for their love of the pragmatic because often nothing else
defines them.

In this sense, they are all madmen and women. Little motivates
them other than the expedient demands of daily survival. There is
not much in their political or social orders that remotely suggests
they understand that our enemy has a desire for how they should
shape their lives and relate to one another.

If "god" exists, for many if not most, it is in their personal lives, but
more often than not this is a projection of their hopes and fears
written onto the universe. We are pleased when the last vestiges
of "god" are found in these private spaces, but the madman still
has the greater part of wisdom. The death of "god" the madman

proclaims may have seemed distant in Nietzsche's time, but it has grown nearer in the present age. We await the full force of this truth to enter into their world.

Consider the voices of those who call them to another way of life, one more in line with our rival's desire. Do they hold sway in the halls of power? Do the prophets construct the economic systems that determine and shape them so definitively? Are the creatures beating their swords into garden hoes, their bombs into energy-producing devices? Are they even taking seriously that there might be another way to live in the world? Outside of those little pockets of resistance that we see pop up from time to time, the evidence seems to suggest not. It is easy for us to marginalize those who keep calling for reconciliation and forgiveness. I don't mind these paragons of wisdom being admired, I just don't want them followed.

And so we wait and watch. We wait to see what they will construct that will reveal the truth of the madman. When they choke on their weapons, when their fear overwhelms their best selves, when the desire for revenge becomes rooted in their DNA, we will be watching. As surely as the earth turns, they can be counted upon to stay the course, and in so doing the madman's wisdom becomes more and more apparent. Their future is hurtling toward them, becoming more and more manifest in its material effects.

Fortunately for us, that future is the one Nietzsche foresaw and not the one our enemy envisions for them. We want them to think that they are getting better and better. In some ways it's true, I suppose, but more sophisticated does not necessarily mean wiser. We want them to think that with enough knowledge they will be able to work their way out of any fix they presently find themselves in. We want them to embrace the myth of progress and fix it into their consciousness, even as they construct bigger bombs and more secure prisons and surveillance states.

Our enemy wants a future of promise for them as well; only the world would look much different if they were to respond to that hope. This would be the world where they would receive all life as a gift and would take their gifts and turn them to ends that lead to the flourishing of earth and its inhabitants.

Opening themselves to the life that sustains them and the holiness found there, they would know through their suffering how deeply they need to make manifest the life of grace. They would become sacraments of grace, lived out in their bodies, embedded within the world. We cannot have that sort of thing. It's unseemly and obnoxious.

Shuffling off that mortal coil of hurts, hates, and resentments, they would live fearless in the world in a way that would immunize them from our desires, plans, and hopes. Called into the hopeful world of our enemy, they would become the mad ones themselves. Mad with love, joy, and peace, they would dance and sing the life still to come into being and the new heaven and the new earth would descend upon them all. Our day would be done, and we must work to ensure that this horrific outcome does not become a reality in their lives. Fortunately for us, so few of them have the heart to see the world with the eyes of grace.

POSTED BY BLZBB AT 11:29 PM, 16/05
TAGS: **DON DRAPER** | **EMPTY SUITS** | **NIETZSCHE,** *THE GAY SCIENCE* |

# Selected Tag Glossary

**1 John 4:18**. "There is no fear in love, but perfect love casts out fear; for fear has to do with punishment, and whoever fears has not reached perfection in love."

**Alexander VI** (1431–1503). One of the most notorious of popes, Alexander, whose real name was Rodrigo Borgia, became known for his nepotism and numerous children. His family name became synonymous with corruption, and his reign was one of the low points in the papacy, though the arts and architecture in Rome flourished under his rule.

**Amos 8:4-6.**
Hear this, you that trample on the needy,
and bring to ruin the poor of the land,
saying, "When will the new moon be over
so that we may sell grain;
and the Sabbath,
so that we may offer wheat for sale?
We will make the ephah small and the shekel great,
and practice deceit with false balances,
buying the poor for silver
and the needy for a pair of sandals,
and selling the sweepings of the wheat."

**ANC.** The acronym for the African National Congress, the political party formed in South Africa to work for the rights of the black South African people and against the practices of apartheid. It was this political party that Nelson Mandela helped to lead until he was imprisoned by the South African government from 1962 until his release from Robben Island in 1990. The most famous member of the ANC, Mandela would become president of South Africa in 1994.

**Anthony of Egypt**. Saint Anthony (251–356) was one of the first and best known of the desert fathers. His biography by Athanasius of Alexandria helped establish the role of monasticism as an important part of the Christian faith. According to the stories Anthony had many struggles with the devil in the desert.

**Aristocentrism**. An inordinate claim of superiority by a society or group of persons.

**Margaret Atwood, *The Handmaid's Tale*.** Fiction work (1985) that tells the story of a theocratic regime in the future. At the end of the book, there is a record of the proceedings of a historical conference studying the Republic of Gilead, which explores, from an academic standpoint, the lives of the people in the novel. The historians, in treating these people's lives in an "objective" fashion, miss the true tragedy of the lives that were ruined by the regime.

**Axial Age**. Term coined by Karl Jaspers to describe the period 800 B.C.E. to 200 B.C.E., when, according to Jaspers, revolutions in religion and philosophy changed the world.

**Babylonian Captivity.** Period of Jewish history (597–538 B.C.E.) during which Jews were taken captive and exiled from the kingdom of Judah to Babylon. Eventually they were allowed to return and reconstruct the second temple in Jerusalem.

**Backstreet Boys**. American pop group formed in Orlando in 1993. They were one of a wave of "boy bands" that were aligned with the Walt Disney Company.

**Jack Bauer**. Character played by Kiefer Sutherland in the television show *24*. The show was controversial because torture became a constant theme of many episodes and led to frequent discussions in American culture about the necessity for torture to stop terrorism. Even some political figures of the neoconservative movement in America used the show as justification for their use of torture.

**Zygmunt Bauman** (1925–). Polish sociologist who explores the connection between modernity and modern bureaucracies in committing atrocity, specifically the Holocaust. Well known for the books *Modernity and the Holocaust* (1989) and *Liquid Modernity* (2000).

**Jeremy Bentham** (1748–1832). English philosopher and jurist who became known for the philosophy of utilitarianism and the concept of the Panopticon. His concept of devising laws for "the greatest good for the greatest number of people" became known as the "greatest happiness principle," or the principle of utility.

**Peter Berger, *The Sacred Canopy***. Berger (1923–), a sociologist of religion, wrote the book *The Sacred Canopy* (1967) to describe the way that religion works to legitimate in a transcendent realm social structures that are transitory and historically located. Though his understanding of the future dominance of secularity over religion would need revision, his observations about the way religion functions to legitimate culture remain insightful and useful in analyzing the role of contemporary religion.

**Ingmar Bergman** (1918–2007). Swedish film director who became famous for films that explore the intersection of religion and existential struggle. His 1957 black-and-white film *The Seventh Seal* is full of images, such as the dance of death and death playing chess on the beach, which have become a source of iconic references in other films.

**Daniel Berrigan** (1921–) **and Philip Berrigan** (1923–2002). The Berrigan brothers were radical priests and social activists who became famous in America in the period of the Vietnam War for resisting the government. Their embrace of pacifism as faithfulness to Jesus Christ led them to start the Plowshares Movement, a movement of social action against the institutionalization of war in government and industry.

**Bharatiya Janata Party.** One of the two major political parties in India, the party is strongly nationalistic and advocates strongly for conservative policies in Indian society. The strong nationalistic orientation has also sometimes led to religiously fueled violence with the Muslim community.

**David Bohm** (1917–1992). A quantum physicist who made significant contributions to the world of physics. Controversial because of his political views, he worked with Albert Einstein at Princeton before moving to Brazil because of problems with the American government. He developed many ideas on thought, neuropsychology, and quantum physics. His concept of an underlying order structuring the patterns of matter and energy remains controversial.

**The Borg**. Characters in the television series *Star Trek: The Next Generation*. They function as a collective of individuals from different cultures who have been conquered and assimilated as cybernetically enhanced drones into the hive mind of the Borg war machine. The Borg do not negotiate or reason; they just conquer and assimilate other races. The tagline of the Borg is "Resistance is futile," which, in popular culture, has become a phrase to address conditions regarding overwhelming force. The Borg is a juggernaut that cannot be stopped.

**British Sky Broadcasting**. One of Rupert Murdoch's many media conglomerates.

**Dan Brown** (1964–). The well-known author of the best-selling book *The Da Vinci Code* (2003). The predecessor to that book was called *Angels and Demons* (2000).

*Caritas in Veritate.* The third papal encyclical of Pope Benedict XVI, it deals with issues of economic justice and global development in modern society. It is a detailed reflection on economic systems and the social order.

**Eric Cartman.** Character in the animated television show *South Park.* In season two, episode 3, Cartman plays a deputized patrol officer whose signature line is "Respect my authoritah!"

**William Cavanaugh,** *Torture and Eucharist.* Cavanaugh is an American theologian who explores in this 1998 book Christian practice in the context of the torture regime of Pinochet in Chile. How Christian faith can resist the move to torture by creating the eucharistic presence of Christ is its main focus.

**Chinvat Bridge.** The Zoroastrian place of judgment where one passes over from life to death. The appearance of the bridge depends on how righteous one was in life. If one's deeds were evil, the bridge would become sharp edged and impossible to stand on. If one was righteous, it becomes a wide and easily navigated path. Respective spirits of horror or honor are also present as tormentors or guides into the next life.

**Noam Chomsky** (1928–). An American linguist, philosopher, and political activist. He has made significant contributions to the field of linguistics and cognitive science, but is better known for his rigorous critique of American public policy. Author of academic books and articles, he wrote the book *Manufacturing Consent: The Political Economy of the Mass Media* (1998), an examination of the connection between contemporary media and propaganda.

**C Street Fellowship.** An outreach of the Fellowship Foundation, the C Street mansion houses members of Congress who share an interest in bringing their faith to bear on public policy. Enormously influential in Washington, D.C., the house became infamous when some of its best-known residents became involved in the sex scandals of Senator John Ensign of Nevada and Governor Mark Sanford of South Carolina. Author Jeff Sharlet exposed some of the ideology and activism of the group in his book *The Family: The Secret Fundamentalism at the Heart of American Power* (2010).

**Dalits.** Self-designation of lower-class persons in Indian society. Through a long history of caste oppression and occupations considered polluting, this community was regarded as "untouchable."

**Hugh Dancy** (1975–). British actor who plays Prince Charmont in the 2004 movie *Ella Enchanted.*

**John Nelson Darby** (1800–1882). Considered the father of a school of thought called dispensationalism, his theological interpretations of apocalyptic themes have been enormously influential in American evangelical circles. Due to his influence, Cyrus Scofield wrote the Scofield Reference Bible, which influenced generations of evangelicals in institutions such as Dallas Theological Seminary. Some of the graduates of this school wrote formative books on the second coming of Jesus Christ. Some scholars contend that he invented the doctrine of the invisible "rapture," which did not appear in Christian teaching previous to him.

**Richard Dawkins** (1941–). An eminent evolutionary biologist whose book *The Selfish Gene* (1976) helped launch a public career. His subsequent books, including *The Blind Watchmaker* (1986) and *The God Delusion* (2006), have given him the reputation of being a type of professional atheist.

**William Dembski** (1960–). Dembski is an American philosopher, mathematician, and theologian. In his numerous books, he has argued for the concept of intelligent design. This states that an intentional mind is at work in the ongoing processes of evolution.

This theory has become one of the avenues that advocates have used to try to put a contemporary form of creationism in public-school systems.

**"Diamonds Are a Girl's Best Friend."** Originally sung in the Broadway musical *Gentleman Prefer Blonds*, this song by Jule Styne and Leo Robin became popular in public consciousness when Marilyn Monroe sang it in the movie of the same name. Many missed the cynical tone of the lyrics, though this is captured well by T-Bone Burnett's version on his album *Trap Door* (1982).

**Annie Dillard, *Pilgrim at Tinker Creek*.** Dillard (1945–) became famous with her publication of *Pilgrim at Tinker Creek*, which won a Pulitzer Prize in 1975. This book contains her observations of nature close to her home in Hollins, Virginia. One of the most compelling images she writes about is the water bug that injects its prey with an enzyme that turns the victim's insides to juice, to be sucked out by the predator for food.

**Discovery Channel Telescope.** Called "The People's Telescope," the Discovery Channel Telescope is being built near Happy Jack, Arizona. The scope will greatly enhance the program of Lowell Observatory in Flagstaff, Arizona. First light is expected in 2012.

**The Discovery Institute.** Not to be confused with the Discovery Channel, the Institute is a think tank located near Seattle, Washington, dedicated to promoting the doctrine of intelligent design (*see* William Dembski). It is dedicated to reversing what they see as a materialist and atheist worldview through education and legal cases.

**Disenchantment.** This term, originally used by the German sociologist Max Weber, was coined to describe a culture that no longer lives under the structuring power of religion, superstition, or mysticism. Modern humanity lives under the domain of rational perspectives and employs science rather than religous beliefs about the world to decide courses of action to take.

**Thomas Dolby** (1958–). British musician best known for his song "She Blinded Me With Science" (1982).

**Fyodor Dostoevsky, *The Brothers Karamazov*.** Dostoevsky (1821–1888) wrote *The Brothers Karamazov* in 1880. In the book, he explores themes of faith, doubt, and the problem of evil. Ivan Karamazov narrates one particularly compelling story in the book to his brother Alyosha. The story, set during the Inquisition, is the story of the Grand Inquisitor who interviews Jesus after he has taken him prisoner. The inquisitor, playing off the temptation narratives of Jesus, raises some difficult and compelling issues concerning human freedom and faith.

**Don Draper.** Main character played by Jon Hamm in the television show *Mad Men*, about an advertising agency in Manhattan in the 1960s.

**Bob Dylan** (1941–). An American music icon who wrote the song "Gotta Serve Somebody" for his 1979 album *Slow Train Coming*.

**Meister Eckhart** (1260–1327). A German mystic who was declared a heretic by the Catholic Church and brought up for trial by Pope John XII. His ideas about faith and religion still elicit fascination among many.

**Edict of Milan.** A letter issued in 313 C.E. by the emperors Constantine and Licinius, proclaiming toleration for Christians in the Roman Empire. It would mark a turning point for the Christian religion and would set off events that would lead later to the Council of Nicaea in 325 C.E.

**Election.** A 1999 movie directed by Alexander Payne about an ambitious high school student (Reese Witherspoon) and the student-government advisor (Matthew Broderick) who attempts to thwart her election as student-body president.

**Enuma Elish.** Babylonian creation epic that tells the story of Marduk and his supremacy in the pantheon of Mesopotamian deities. Various dates of origin have been proposed; however, many scholars believe it dates to the Bronze Age, around the eighteenth to sixteenth centuries B.C.E.

**Fibonacci Sequences.** A mathematical formulation of integers found in the following sequence, 0, 1, 1, 2, 3, 5, 8, 13, 21, 34, 55, 89, 144, . . . Used in a variety of ways, the mathematical formulation is found in the world of nature (pine cones, sea shells, even leopard's spots) and also used in the analysis of financial markets.

**Michel Foucault** (1926–1984). A French philosopher who critiqued social institutions such as prisons and psychiatry. He dealt extensively with the way in which government and other institutions work to control social life. His work looks at the dynamics of power and knowledge in how society constructs itself. Labeled as a postmodernist, he was uncomfortable being pigeonholed into a school of thought.

**Four Noble Truths.** One of the fundamental pillars of Buddhist teachings, the truths are the revelation the Buddha received as he mediated in search of enlightenment. The truths, expressed simply, say, all life is suffering; suffering is caused by desire; stop the desire, stop the suffering; and desire can be mitigated by following the eightfold path, which are prescriptions for living a balanced life.

**Sigmund Freud, *The Future of an Illusion*.** Freud (1856–1934) was the founder of psychoanalysis. His 1927 book, *The Future of an Illusion*, is a critique of religion in which he contends that religion is a projection of humankind's fears, desires, and other psychological needs. God, he argues, turns out exactly like something we would envision to meet our needs, especially the fear of death.

**Thomas Friedman** (1953–). *New York Times* columnist and author of several books that deal with global problems. In an interview with Charlie Rose after the beginning of the Iraq War in 2001, he justified the invasion of Iraq by saying that American forces needed to go into the homes of our enemies and tell them America was not going to stand for being attacked. His statement ended with the phrase "Well. Suck. On. This."

**Giant Water Bug.** *See* Annie Dillard.

**Mel Gibson** (1956–). Australian actor who directed the 2004 film *The Passion of the Christ*, noted especially for its graphically violent depiction of Christ's suffering and crucifixion.

***The Grifters.*** A 1990 film directed by Stephen Frears, starring John Cusack, Annette Bening, and Anjelica Huston, about con artists and the way that the con distorts human relationships.

**Hugo Grotius** (1583–1645). A Dutch philosopher, theologian, and jurist who formulated concepts of natural rights and law. He laid the foundations for international law. Though he was religious himself, when it came to setting up international law, he argued that humans should do it *etsi deus non daretur* ("as if God did not exist"). This concept became connected to Dietrich Bonhoeffer and his prison writings.

**Gush Emunim.** An ultranational and right-wing Israeli messianic and political movement formed in 1974 in response to the Yom Kippur War of 1974, though it has history that extends back to the Six Days War of 1967. Rooted in the teachings of Rabbi Abraham

Issac Kook and his son, Tzvi Yehuda Kook, the movement is committed to reclaiming through settlement, or other means, land on the West Bank and Gaza they believe is part of the land God promised Israel in Hebrew Scripture. They believe that the retaking of this land will hasten the arrival of the Jewish messiah.

**Ted Haggard** (1956–). An American evangelist who became enormously important in the evangelical world, serving as the leader of the National Association of Evangelicals from 2003 to 2006. In 2006, a male prostitute claimed that Haggard had paid him for three years to have sex and that Haggard had taken crystal methamphetamine in these sessions. Haggard resigned his positions shortly thereafter.

**Stuart Hameroff** (1947–). Anesthesiologist and professor at the University of Arizona who became interested in human consciousness and serves as Director of Consciousness Studies in Tucson, Arizona. His theories of consciousness focus on the role of microtubules and quantum computation.

**Anne Hathaway** (1982–). American actress who plays Ella of Frell in the 2004 movie *Ella Enchanted*.

**Mark Heard** (1951–1992). Singer-songwriter who recorded music mostly in the contemporary Christian genre. One of the songs off his 1982 album *Victims of the Age* was titled "Everybody Loves a Holy War," a searing indictment of religion as a tool for justifying war.

**Christopher Hitchens** (1949–). A social and literary critic who has worked as a public intellectual in politics, literary criticism, and religion. In recent years, he has found himself dealing more with religion, as in his 2007 book *God Is Not Great: How Religion Poisons Everything*. Regarded as one of the fathers (along with

Richard Dawkins) of the new atheism movement, he was diagnosed with esophageal cancer in 2010.

**Hutus.** A Central African ethnic tribal community who orchestrated the Rwandan genocide against the Tutsi, another ethnic community with whom they had been in conflict, especially acute since Belgium's colonization of the area in the twentieth century.

**IMF.** Acronym for the International Monetary Fund, an international organization that oversees global financial matters. Often criticized for the control it exerts over countries.

***Inception.*** A 2010 movie directed by Christopher Nolan, starring Leonardo di Caprio and Ellen Page. It ostensibly deals with the world of dreams and consciousness; however, there are as many interpretations of this film as there are of another movie that dealt with consciousness, *The Matrix* (1999).

**Indian National Congress Party.** One of the two major political parties in India. One of the largest democratic parties in the world, they are led by Sonia Gandhi and Manmohan Singh.

**Irenaeus of Lyons** (second century C.E.–202). He was one of the first theologians of the Christian faith, best known for his attack on Gnosticism. In his writings on creation and the fall, he places perfection as a goal in the future, not something lost in the past. This became a minority opinion in the Christian faith as the narrative of loss and exile came to define Christian perspectives about the early Genesis passages.

**Inspector Javert.** Law-and-order-obsessed character who pursues Jean Valjean, the protagonist in Victor Hugo's *Les Misérables*.

**Janis Joplin** (1943–1970). Singer who died tragically at a young age of a heroin overdose. One of her most famous songs was "Me and Bobby McGee," written by Kris Kristofferson, which includes the line, "Freedom's just another word for nothin' left to lose."

**Dr. Jan Karski** (1914–2000). A Polish resistance fighter in World War II who reported to the Allies the conditions of Jews in Warsaw. He was smuggled into the Warsaw ghetto by Jews so they could show him the truth of what was really going on. In 1982, Yad Vashem recognized him as Righteous Among the Nations for his work in alerting the world to the treatment of Jews.

***Kitzmiller v. Dover.*** The first case brought against a school district for requiring the teaching of intelligent design as an alternative to evolution. The plaintiffs argued that intelligent design was a form of creationism and thus should not be taught in the public school system. Their argument was upheld in the United States District Court for the Middle District of Pennsylvania in 2005.

**Kris Kristofferson** (1936–). Singer-songwriter who wrote the 1969 song "Me and Bobby McGee." *See* Janis Joplin.

**Thomas Kuhn, *The Structure of Scientific Revolutions.*** Kuhn (1922–1996) was an American physicist who wrote on the history and philosophy of science. His 1962 book *The Structure of Scientific Revolutions* argues that science does not proceed in a linear fashion in the acquisition of knowledge, but goes through paradigm shifts, periodic revolutions in which the nature of science changes. One of the things he pointed to is the subjectivity in science.

**Tim LaHaye and Jerry Jenkins.** Authors of the "Left Behind" series of books that deals extensively in a dispensationalist perspective regarding the return of Christ. These books have had enormous influence in shaping the consciousness of a new generation around the narrative of dispensationalist thinking (*see* John Nelson Darby).

**Lancaster County.** Lancaster County in Pennsylvania is the epicenter of the Amish community in America. West Nickel Mines School is located in Bart Township of Lancaster County.

***Lebensraum.*** German for "living space" or "habitat." This was one of the guiding ideas of Nazi ideology, argued by Adolf Hitler in the book *Mein Kampf* (My Struggle) (1925–1926). It was a perspective that said the German people had the right to expand their territory and take the land and resources of those who were deemed inferior (*see* aristocentricism).

***Les Misérables.*** Book written by Victor Hugo in 1862 that deals with several characters over a seventeen-year period in France. Exploring the themes of law, grace, and redemption in a setting of revolution and class warfare, it has become popular in contemporary consciousness as a musical.

**Hal Lindsey** (1929–). Author of one of the most popular books of dispensationalist apocalypticism, *The Late, Great Planet Earth*, in 1970. This book continued the dispensationalist stream of thinking in many evangelicals. It has sold more than thirty-five million copies.

**John Locke** (1632–1704). An English philosopher who is considered one of the pillars of the Enlightenment. Sometimes called the father of liberalism, his work in social-contract theory was crucial in the thinking of the American founding documents. Locke laid the foundations of the modern state.

**Archibald MacLeish, *JB*.** MacLeish (1892–1982) wrote the play *JB* in 1956 as an update to the Job story found in Jewish Scripture.

**Marduk.** Babylonian name of ancient God and patron deity of the city of Babylon. *See Enuma Elish.*

**The Matrix.** A 1999 movie by the Wachowski brothers starring Keanu Reeves, Carrie-Anne Moss, and Laurence Fishburne. The film deals with themes of consciousness and reality set in an apocalyptic future.

**Maya.** In Hindu thought, Maya represents the deception and illusion that needs to be seen through to achieve release from the wheel of samsara, the circle of death and rebirth. This life is transitory and ephemeral, not true existence, which is Brahman.

**John Milton, *Paradise Lost*.** Originally published in 1667 by Milton (1608–1674), *Paradise Lost* is an epic poem in blank verse that deals with the fall of humankind found in the Genesis story. The text claimed the imaginations of many people and became a part of the formation of Western consciousness regarding the Genesis narrative and its views of Satan.

**Thomas More, *Utopia*.** More (1478–1535) wrote the 1516 book *Utopia* (literally "no place"), which depicts an island where the contrast between an idyllic community of equality and religious toleration and the world of sixteenth-century Europe is stark. There are many different interpretations offered for why More wrote the book, but the island of Utopia became well known in the sixteenth century and beyond.

**Neo.** Character played by Keanu Reeves in the 1999 movie *The Matrix*.

**Neocons.** Short term for neoconservatives, a group of American political actors who were ascendant in the presidency of George W. Bush. They were the motivating force behind the Project for a New American Century, an agenda for American foreign and domestic policy for the twenty-first century. Irving Kristol, often called the founder of neoconservatism, and his son, William Kristol, have been the intellectual anchors of this movement. Led by persons such as Dick Cheney and Donald Rumsfeld, the neoconservatives guided American foreign policy in the wake of the September 11, 2001, attacks.

**Friedrich Nietzsche, *The Gay Science*.** Nietzsche (1844–1900) wrote the book *The Gay Science* in 1882. It contains the parable of the Madman.

***O Tannenbaum*.** German title of the song "O Christmas Tree."

**Panentheism.** Theological perspective that combines pantheist and theist elements to contend that the life of God interpenetrates both material and spiritual life. Whereas pantheism argues that God is the whole, panentheism says the whole is *in* God. God is not confined to material life, but the life of God extends beyond it. One of the metaphors used to explain this has been the world is the body of God, but God is the consciousness and mind of the universe.

**Panopticon.** The Panopticon was first proposed as a type of prison by Jeremy Bentham. It was designed so that the jailer could observe all the prisoners at one time, but the prisoners did not know they were being watched. Bentham said this was an extension of power unknown to human beings at the time. Recently it has served as a metaphor of state power and the surveillance state. Presently some see the modern state assuming the power of omniscience. *See* Michel Foucault.

**Parliament of the World's Religion.** Begun in 1893 at the Chicago World's Fair, the Parliament of the World's Religions was created "to cultivate harmony among the world's religious and spiritual communities and foster their engagement with the world and its guiding institutions in order to achieve a just, peaceful and sustainable world."

***The Passion of the Christ.*** *See* Mel Gibson.

**Phish.** Led by Trey Anastasio, Phish is an American jam band, known for extended jams, devout fans, and free-form dancing.

**Steven Pinker** (1954–). Evolutionary psychologist and linguist who has become known for his work in cognitive sciences and the formation of languages. He is aligned with the Daniel Dennett and Richard Dawkins perspectives regarding evolutionary adaptations.

**Plymouth Brethren.** Conservative evangelical group begun in Dublin, Ireland, in 1820. Their doctrine was intensely dispensational and premillenial. John Nelson Darby, father of the modern rapture doctrine, was a part of this group.

**Polycarp, Bishop of Smyrna** (69–155). One of the first recorded Christian martyrs.

**Billy Preston** (1946–2006). An American rhythm-and-blues singer and keyboardist who moved among rock royalty in the 1960s and '70s, most notably the Beatles. One of his most popular songs was "Will It Go 'Round in Circles?" (1973).

**W. V. Quine** (1908–2000). A mathematician and analytical philosopher who made contributions to the philosophy of science, especially to the epistemology of how we can do science from the paucity of sensory evidence.

**Ayn Rand, *Atlas Shrugged.*** Rand (1905–1982) wrote the 1957 book *Atlas Shrugged* as an apology for her philosophy of objectivism. It tells the story of John Galt, leader of a strike by the intelligentsia in American society. According to the narrative, the most creative and brilliant minds in American society become fed up supporting those lower on the pyramid and withdraw until society has reorganized itself. This book and Rand's philosophy of self-interest and ethical egoism have become highly regarded in American libertarianism and ultra-conservatism. Former Federal Reserve Chairman, Alan Greenspan, was deeply involved with the movement surrounding Rand.

**John Rawls** (1921–2002). American philosopher who developed theories of justice. He appeals to a number of traditions of liberalism (social contract, principle of fairness) to argue for principles of egalitarian social justice and behavior.

**Realpolitik.** Roughly translates into politics done on the basis of power in the cause of practical or material affairs and not done on the basis of ethics or political theory. For many who subscribe to this ideology, politics should be managed on what exists in the "real" world.

**The Reverend Ike** (1935–2009). Evangelist of the prosperity school. One of his most famous lines was, "It is the lack of money that is the root of all evil."

**Rolling Stones, "Sympathy for the Devil."** Song off of the 1968 Rolling Stones album *Beggars Banquet.* Sung in the voice of Satan, the song contains lyrics that state, "Pleased to meet you, hope you guessed my name."

**Holmes Rolston III** (1932– ). Winner of the 2003 Templeton Prize. He has written numerous books on religion and science and uses the metaphor that the world is the eros of God, indicating God's great passion for the world.

**Oscar Romero** (1917–1980). The Roman Catholic archbishop of El Salvador during the height of their civil war (1977–1980).

As archbishop, he became aware of the immense suffering of the Salvadoran people at the hands of the oligarchy. When he took steps to address the social injustices of his country, he was assassinated while offering the Eucharist on March 24, 1980. He has a place on the wall of martyrs at Westminster Abbey in London.

**Richard Rorty** (1931–2007). An American philosopher who forged a new philosophy of pragmatism based on the realization that people are always formulating language and ideas in social locations that vary over time. In *Philosophy and the Mirror of Nature* (1979), he argues that the whole idea of foundationalist epistemology is mistaken.

**Jean-Jacques Rousseau, *Émile*.** Rousseau (1712–1778) was a political philosopher and another pillar of the Enlightenment who helped lay the foundations for modern liberalism. He would become identified with the worst expressions of the French Revolution because he was embraced by so many of its proponents. His 1762 book, *Émile*, was an exploration of human nature, education, and the role of society on moral and spiritual development.

**J. K. Rowling** (1965–). The author of the "Harry Potter" series of books. In 2000, she was awarded with the Order of the British Empire for her work.

**Paul Rusesabagina** (1954–). The subject of the movie *Hotel Rwanda* concerning his actions during the Rwandan genocide. He was credited with saving 1,268 refugees from the violence that swept the country in 1994.

**Samsara.** This is the doctrine of the wheel of rebirth in Hinduism. Humans are caught on the wheel of reincarnation until they can achieve moksha, release from the wheel of brith, death, and rebirth.

**C. I. Scofield** (1843–1921). Scofield was a colorful figure in American religious history. Plagued by scandal, he would eventually write the Scofield Reference Bible, one of the most circulated Bibles in American evangelicalism. Steeped heavily in the theology of John Nelson Darby, this commentary on the Bible solidified for many the teachings of dispensationalism, the rapture, and the premillenial expectation of Christ's return.

***The Seventh Seal.*** *See* Ingmar Bergman.

**Shoah.** Shoah is another word to designate the Holocaust suffered by Jews during World War II. It is also the name of a 1985 movie by Claude Lanzmann about the Holocaust.

**Smashing Pumpkins, "Disarm."** A song by the American rock group on the 1993 album *Siamese Dream*. It contains the lyric, "The killer in me is the killer in you."

**Adam Smith, *The Wealth of Nations*.** Shorthand for a book published by Adam Smith (1723–1790) in 1776, *The Wealth of Nations* is a treatise on economics arguing that enlightened and rational self-interest along with competition can lead to economic prosperity. Though he mentions the concept elsewhere, he used the term "the invisible hand" to indicate forces that are at work in structures of which we may not be immediately aware. The term is still in use today among some economists.

***South Park.*** Animated television series that features four wildly profane little boys, Stan, Kyle, Eric, and Kenny.

**Britney Spears** (1981–). An American entertainer, she got her start in show business with Disney as a part of the Mickey Mouse Club. *See* Backstreet Boys.

**Barbra Streisand, "The Way We Were."** Sung as part of the 1973 movie of the same title, the song "The Way We Were" by Alan and Marilyn Bergman contains the lyrics, "Memories may be beautiful and yet, what's too painful to remember we simply choose to forget."

**Tamil Tigers**. A separatist group of guerilla fighters in Sri Lanka that used violence to overthrow the government of Sri Lanka. In May of 2009, the government seemed finally to end the organization.

**Tertullian** (160–220). An early Christian apologist and theologian. One of the first theologians to use the word *Trinity*, he was also famous for the line, "The blood of the martyrs is the seed of the church."

**André and Magda Trocmé.** André Trocmé (1901–1971) was a pastor in a remote French village at the start of the invasion by Germany. Early on in his career, he was sent to the remote village of Le Chambon because of his pacifist views. He spoke out early against discrimination against the Jews and urged his congregation and other ministers to shelter the Jewish community from the Nazis and the Vichy government. As a result of André's efforts, Le Chambon and the surrounding areas became a rare haven for the Jews. Yad Vashem not only recognized Trocmé and his wife, Magda, as righteous but also the entire village of Le Chambon, the only village so honored.

**Tina Turner** (1939–). American singer who had a hit with the 1984 song "What's Love Got to Do With It?"

**Tutsis.** A Central African ethnic group that was attacked and massacred by Hutu members of a rival tribe in the Rwandan genocide of 1994.

**United Healthcare.** One of the largest providers of health-related insurance plans in America.

**Miroslav Volf, *Exclusion and Embrace*.** Born in Croatia, Volf (1956–) is one of the most influential theologians in contemporary times. *Christianity Today* selected his 1996 book *Exclusion and Embrace* as one of the one hundred best religious books of the twentieth century. The book deals with societal conflict and the means of dealing with it through Christian disciplines of forgiveness and reconciliation.

**Max Weber** (1864–1920). A German sociologist who had a significant impact on social theory. Most famous for his 1905 book *The Protestant Ethic and the Spirit of Capitalism*, he also defined the modern state as an entity that claims a monopoly on the use of violence. One of his most intriguing images is that of the iron cage, by which he meant the increasing rationalization of social life. We become trapped in the prisons we have created by modern technology and bureaucracy. *See* Zygmunt Bauman.

**West Nickel Mines School**. The West Nickel Mines School was the site of the slaughter of five Amish children in 2006.

**Zazen.** The practice of sitting mediation in Zen Buddhism.

**Slavoj Žižek** (1949–). A Slovenian philosopher and social theorist who works with the thought of Jacques Lacan and psychoanalysis to interpret contemporary life. In recent years, he has turned his attention to political theology, interpreting religious themes from the viewpoint of atheism

**Émile Zola** (1840–1902). A French writer who became involved in the Dreyfus affair when he wrote a stunning article in the paper *L'Aurore*, which contained the headline *J'Accuse!* In the article, Zola accused the highest levels of the French government and military of falsifying and hiding evidence that proved Alfred Dreyfus was innocent of charges of espionage. In doing this, he was exposing the anti-Semitism that led to Dreyfus being unfairly accused by the government.